W9-AQB-865

Sleepaway School

Sleepaway School

Stories from a Boy's Life

Lee Stringer

SEVEN STORIES PRESS

New York • London • Toronto • Melbourne

A Seven Stories Press First Edition

The author wishes to thank the Writers League Fund for their generous support during a critical time during the writing of this book.

Seven Stories Press
140 Watts Street
New York, NY 10013
http://www.sevenstories.com/

IN CANADA
Publishers Group Canada, 250A Carlton Street, Toronto, ON M5A 2L1

IN THE UK
Turnaround Publisher Services Ltd., Unit 3, Olympia Trading Estate, Coburg Road, Wood Green, London N22 6TZ

IN AUSTRALIA
Palgrave Macmillan, 627 Chapel Street, South Yarra VIC 3141

LIBRARY OF CONGRESS CATALOGING-IN-PUBLICATION DATA
Stringer, Lee.
Sleepaway school : stories from a boy's life / Lee Stringer.—
A Seven Stories Press 1st ed.
p. cm.
ISBN 1-58322-478-5 (hardcover : alk. paper)
1. Stringer, Lee.
2. Problem children—United States—Biography.
3. Hawthorne-Cedar Knolls School. I. Title.
HQ773.S76 2004
649'.153'092—dc22
2004003610

College professors may order examination copies of Seven Stories Press titles for a free six-month trial period. To order, visit www.sevenstories.com/textbook/ or fax on school letterhead to 212.226.1411.

Book design by India Amos, based on a design by Adam Simon

Printed in the USA

9 8 7 6 5 4 3 2 1

For my mother, Elizabeth Phoebe Treadwell

Contents

Foreword by Kurt Vonnegut ix

Preface xi

1 Three fatherless sons walking . . . 1

2 The thing is . . . 5

3 At the back of the lot . . . 9

4 My mother has a Victrola . . . 15

5 When the cops get to . . . 21

6 I do just as the cops say . . . 25

7 The next morning . . . 31

8 We're all in the auditorium . . . 35

9 It's a Friday . . . 45

10 First, there is . . . 51

11 For most of its history . . . 57

12 They are short one . . . 63

13 We're in the van . . . 73

14 My mother brings along . . . 81

15 . . . Our day . . . 89

16 They took me . . . 95

17 All of us . . . 101

18 Every Tuesday . . . 107

19 This new kid. This Walter . . . 113

20 Red-haired . . . 119

21 Steve has pictures. Sexy pictures . . . 123

22 Curiosity and urgency . . . 127

23 I've begun to halfways suspect . . . 131

24 I think it's stepping back . . . 141

25 If I peer through . . . 149

26 I don't go back . . . 157

27 A week before . . . 163
28 On the inside . . . 171
29 We're down . . . 177
30 The flu . . . 183
31 It's around midnight, and . . . 193
32 A Friday . . . 201
33 Princess . . . 211
34 There's a big . . . 219
About the Author 227

Foreword

This all really happened to the author, and so must be called a memoir rather than a work of fiction. And the real life so described is still going on. The memoirist Lee Stringer, baptismal first name "Caverly," is at the time of its publication one hell of a good writer, and only fifty-four. This is his second book, the first, the huge critical success *Grand Central Winter* (1998), having been about the adventures of his American soul while riding around inside the body of a crack addict in New York City, listening with the addict's ears, looking out through the addict's eyes.

In this new one, the soul of the writer-to-be is riding around inside the body of an always fatherless, occasionally violent, African-American adolescent whose mother is on welfare. He has been living with his mother and brother and going to public school in a mostly white and prosperous suburb of New York City.

And the author still lives in that suburb, his hometown after all. Yes, and I have just spoken to him on the telephone. We have been friends ever since I was so publicly wowed by his first memoir. And I told him that he had achieved universality with *Sleepaway School*, despite how strikingly particular the details of his life had been. He had done it, I said, by writing what Germans call a *Bildungsroman*. I spelled it for him and explained that a tale so-named is about the education and physical development of a human being during the very few years in which he or she stops being a child and becomes an adult.

Some miracle! What a glorious and perfectly awful and *universal* ordeal!

In *Sleepaway School*, a boy becomes a man. The way Lee Stringer tells it, that is by itself more than enough for an enthralling story. Never mind which boy, never mind the milieu, although the boy and the milieu can in their own right be called *really something.*

Kurt Vonnegut
New York City
February 27, 2004

Preface

Somewhere in there, not long after I had gotten my kid's legs under me and had begun to walk myself to and fro, it was determined by those who are charged with knowing such things that I was what we today would call a "child at risk." It was an unsettling thing—seeing such concern etched upon so many grownup faces. And it had the rude effect of acquainting me, far, far too soon, with doubt. But they were right. We wee people were all at risk. Every mother's son of us. Even those of us with overflowing larders and soft, warm beds. Our young hearts like leaves in the wind, we all had to face down the inner turmoil of being, simply, children. We were all on shaky ground.

1

Three fatherless sons walking down Palmer Avenue, avoiding the cracks in the pavement. Skipping ahead to kick at small stones. The year is 1961. We head for the big empty lot across the street from my house. For ten magical days every other year, this is the staging ground of the Clyde Beatty Circus. Ten days of horse dung and cotton candy flavoring the air. Ten nights of barkers and hurdy-gurdy music to put me off to sleep and color my dreams—all of it practically right outside my window.

This summer it's the off year, but we've found our fun on the lot nonetheless. We took Okinawa there in a brave and glorious charge one sunny afternoon. Our dry, mud-clump grenades exploding splendidly against the rocks and trees. The same tall maples from whose high branches we swung like monkeys and thumped our chests and screamed ourselves hoarse one Saturday. After watching a *Tarzan* double-bill matinee at the Playhouse Theater, I got so carried away I lost my footing and took a hard plunge. A good twenty feet to the ground, too. Such is the magic of summer, though, I didn't hit a single branch.

Another day we ventured to the lot's farther reaches. On the other side of the railroad tracks we stumbled across a hidden rubbish heap upon which marvelous toys once owned by children of better fortune were prematurely laid to rest. I dug a perfectly good Remco wind-up arcade game out of the rubble and spent hours of alone time with the thing. Belly-down in the yard, one eye cocked down the sight of its plastic BB gun, picking one tin duck after another off the rotating wheel. Michael found himself a toy fire truck. It was missing a front tire, but the water pump and hose still worked, just like the real thing. I don't remember what Chuck found. If anything.

Michael and Chuck are the only friends I have made since my mother moved my brother and me here from the Bronx five years ago. I remember stepping off the train when we arrived and glimpsing down from the platform at the sleepy, untroubled little town below, how it felt a little like we were immigrants, like we had landed in America for the first time—the tidy, three-story, back-roads America that beams out from the pages of so many picture magazines, down whose tree-lined, picket-fenced, small-town streets so many Hollywood movie cameras have lovingly crawled, the Norman Rockwell, Frank Capra America. In which the pursuit of happiness is a most sacred thing. And indeed I felt that nothing but happiness would follow.

Once I started at school, though, and began rubbing shoulders with other people's sons and daughters, the feeling soon lost its blush. It was different back in the Bronx, where I went to kindergarten. My teacher was always going on about how well I got along with the other kids. I certainly didn't know why anyone wouldn't be good at this. What else was there for a kid but to make new friends? Walking up to someone new and saying, "Hi, my name is so and so, what's yours?" was like a fresh adventure each time. Next thing you knew you'd made a new friend and the world was that much bigger.

The kids here, though, are not as open as all that. Walk up and say *what's your name* and it seems to throw them. They can't wait to shrink away and be rid of you. At least that's the way it's been for me. Not so much a landing, anymore. More like we have invaded or intruded upon something that's already complete and satisfied without need nor room nor inclination for further variation.

I met Michael first. His house was right next door to mine. Hidden from the street by a stand of hedges nearly eight feet tall. It was a tiny place. A former hot dog stand I have been told. There was barely room enough inside for him and his mother. He was standing at the head of his gravel driveway. Not waiting or looking for anyone. Just perfectly content, it seemed, to stand in one spot. I introduced myself. Told him I had just moved next door. And we kicked around for a while in the huge lumber lot that was his back yard. It was great. I scurried home afterwards. Told my mother in a breathless gush about having made a new friend.

"Is he chocolate or vanilla?" she wanted to know.

I told her "Chocolate," when I caught her drift.

She smiled and said, "That's nice."

Michael and I were at the school playground one Saturday spinning ourselves nauseous on the merry-go-round when we spotted Chuck moping down the way. There was something so lonesome about him I thought nothing of calling him over to play with us. My mother's eyes went wide this time, when I answered that this new friend was vanilla.

"I betcha *they* got money," she said.

We take the long route. Walk to the light at the corner first, having been endlessly cautioned against crossing in the middle of the block. Palmer Avenue is a pretty busy street for a small town like Mamaroneck. It can be dangerous at times. Two years ago, when I was nine, I got hit by a car for crossing it at the wrong place. Me and my brother, Wayne, had just peeked into an ambulance parked up the block. It was Wayne's idea. I don't really like ambulances. They strike me as death wagons. But Wayne has a quiet kind of curiosity that sends him suddenly to this place or that. So I went along.

We went up the block, where Wayne had seen it parked. Darted across the street. Pressed our faces against the rear window and peered inside. It gave me the willies. The bare stretcher laying there. The ominous green oxygen tank standing ready beside it. The compartments and boxes marked with red crosses. I couldn't wait to get out of there. And when we were done I rushed into the street without looking. I didn't see the car. Or hear it coming. Just Wayne yelling, "Look out," then . . . blackness.

A few minutes later I found myself sitting at the edge of a neighbor's high lawn. My feet dangling over the wall. A serious-looking man was holding something soft against the back of my throbbing head. Beside him was a little black bag. The magic of summer again. I had gotten struck down right in front of a doctor's house of all places.

When we reach the corner—where Palmer intersects with Rockland—there isn't a car in sight. But the traffic light decides to put up a big red grin for spite. And time seems to come to a halt as we wait for the green. Time is funny that way. Collapsing down to an instant during life's most delicious portions. Ballooning up to near infinity when things are at a dull throb. Summer seems to defy this rule. Always a long, lazy, seemingly endless sprawl. A vacation, in a way, from the tyranny of time itself.

Yet this summer is evaporating with alarming speed. Already the flatter, more sober light of fall has started to seep into the afternoons. Soon it will be Labor Day. Soon summer will be over with. And soon after that they will come for me.

2

The thing is, I did fine in school at first. Until the third grade at least. It wasn't a happy thing going there every day. But I filled my report cards with esses. For *Satisfactory*. Then one afternoon I was leaving the building after classes and standing in the doorway, leaning against the frame, was a kid named Richard. Lucky Richard to me. I had seen him in passing mostly. Strutting down the corridors. Hobnobbing with friends in the cafeteria. Darting around the playground. Yet even in these stolen glimpses it could be seen. In the cut and fabric of his clothes. In his all-American good looks—the kind of looks that buy you an easier time of it all around—in the careless confidence of the very breaths he drew. That Richard was numbered among the luckier sons of this world. Those who seem to fit in so perfectly. And who move around so freely and effortlessly within what seems to be the natural order of things, you can't help but half suspect God himself is on their side.

To this day I do not remember throwing the punch. Just a millisecond, maybe, of blankness. Nothing more than the space of an eyeblink, really. More like a sneeze than anything else. I only remember drawing my fist back from Richard's face. Seeing the twin rivulets of blood trailing down his upper lip. Him gaping at me wide-eyed. Wondering why it had gotten into me to bash in his aquiline nose and despoil his perfectly pressed shirt.

I was as shocked as he was. I had never in my life thrown a punch at anyone. Slamming your fist into someone has always struck me as such a personal violation. Outrageous, and conspicuous, too. I have never been able to convince myself, in the instant between the impulse and the actual act, that anyone ever deserves it. Much less that I could ever deserve to be the one to dish it out. Yet for some reason some something in me had just cracked this kid dead in the face.

We stood there. Almost toe to toe. Each stunned. As if we both had just been mugged by some third person. Stood there panting into each other's faces. I remember this precisely. Lucky Richard's breath on my cheek. Remember it feeling like a prize finally won.

The principal, Mr. Gingrich, flew out of the building. And right behind him the gym teacher. They both grimaced when they saw me, still coiled in a boxer's pose. Then gave me their backs and hovered over Richard, dusted him off, tilted his head back, put a handkerchief to his rudely abused nose. Asked him calmly and gently whatever, by God, had happened. To my surprise Richard didn't scream or sneer, or cry, or accuse. Just shrugged and answered, with precise honesty, "I don't know."

The gym teacher glared righteous fire at me as he led Richard inside. A look that left me feeling like some sort of germ. Then Mr. Gingrich turned to me, his brows high on his balding head and asked, with exasperation on his breath, why I had done what I had done.

As if I knew.

Maybe it was just that it was a Thursday.

Thursday afternoons we had social studies. And for the last three weeks or so we'd been working our way through the 1700s and 1800s. A time of two very separate stories, to hear our history primers tell it. On the one hand, the Europeans. A whole parade of them. Stalwart men and women all. Each captains of their own fortunes. On the other hand, the Africans. The slave ships. The plantations. The North. The South. The Civil War. The Negro. A heritage all too stingy on the kind of valor, honor, courage and greatness that seemed to amply color all the rest of recorded history. All it did was make me squirm. It reeked of a lowliness with which I had no interest in being associated.

That particular Thursday had been the squirmiest yet. Not only because we were reading aloud in turn. A thing that drove me buggy.

Having to suffer through the slower kids who can barely make out half the words, much less give them the flavor or nuance they obviously require. My eyes wandered out the window. And when I pulled them back in I noticed that the attention of several of my classmates had found its way to the back of the room, to where I had always sat beyond particular notice, their eyes making a shy but sly survey of me.

I thought there was a booger on my nose or something at first. Then, looking down at my textbook, at the bottom of the page, I saw the Currier & Ives illustration, a depiction of a creature barely recognizable as human. His limbs, lips, cheekbones and crown out of all proportion. Shrouded in filthy rags. And stretched across a pile of hay. Fast asleep. While in the background a handful of other people toiled away. A pair of smirking, fair-haired boys loomed over him, making a sport of trying to push a piece of straw into his grotesquely gaping nostrils. Below this the caption read simply, "*Negro Slave.*"

My face caught fire when I realized the connection my classmates were drawing between the guy in the picture and me. Worse than that, though, was what the picture seemed to confirm. That it is after all a *them* and *us*, chocolate and vanilla, world. A Norman Rockwell world for *them* and this Currier & Ives world for *us*.

So, maybe that was it. Maybe that was what I was carrying with me when I headed for the door that afternoon. Whatever it was, it clicked something in me I never knew was there. I mean I didn't even know Richard, really. Never had anything in the least against the guy. I would have flushed with gratitude had he ever made the merest overture of friendship towards me, to tell the truth. Yet in that moment, glimpsing him there, leaning in the doorway, hands in his pockets, eyes at half-mast, his brow as clear and untroubled as a spring afternoon, some terrible, primal thing in me could not for a second longer abide his utter casualness.

Mr. Gingrich, as plump and balding and amiable as any Norman Rockwell principal, drew his forefinger like a stubby, pink gun and wagged it before me. *"No, no,"* I heard him saying. *"This will not do. It will not do at all!"* I hung my head. Peered over the toes of my shoes at the blood on the ground, a dark stain on the bright, sunlit concrete. And I had to agree. It certainly wouldn't do.

3

At the back of the lot, Rockland Avenue rises into a bridge over the railroad tracks. We peer west down the track bed to where it converges on infinity. There is always the possibility of a train in the distance. A chance to scramble onto the tracks for a quick game of *chicken*—vying to be the very last one to leap off as the train comes hurling towards you. We peer in the other direction, the view framed by the tunnel of shadow cast by the bridge. But there is nothing. Only the far, narrow horizon quivering languidly under the heat of the sun.

Then I see it. Under the bridge, perched at a tilt on the slope: a large, brown paper bag, the kind you get at the supermarket. A promising bulge in its sides. I go over, give the thing a kick with the toe of my sneakers, and it rolls down the slope a little. As it does, a smaller, clear plastic bag separates itself.

In it I see pinkness.

I see little feet.

I see . . . tiny toes!

"Look," I say, "a doll!"

But as soon as I say this I see it has its thumb in its mouth. And there is something long, stringy and altogether grisly coiled around its throat.

Michael moves up and peers at the thing.

We sometimes call him "Fish" when he isn't looking because he has huge, fleshy lips. He also has skin dark and glossy as polished walnuts. And a head of fine, tightly curled, black hair. Which combination will account for his eventually growing into a strikingly handsome young man. But as kids, we only notice his lips.

". . . S'not a doll," he says. And there is something about his eyes. They seem stuck there when he says it. "'Sa *premature embryo.* 'Sgot the *umbilical cord* around its neck."

He's so calm saying this it's almost scary.

Michael has been reading books, I tell myself.

Chuck inches up. Gives a quick sidewise glance at the thing and shrinks back. We don't have a nickname for Chuck. Despite that he is a collection of squares. Square shoulders. Square head. Square black frame glasses.

"God," Chuck says, and it makes me think of God. Of the picture of Him my mother keeps on the mantel above the fireplace. One of those trick pictures you get at Woolworth's. The eyes follow you no matter what angle you peer at it from. It's one of the reasons why even in winter I spend so much time out of doors. It spooks me, Him forever peering down from on high. Always watching. As if He's just waiting for me to slip up. So he can fry me in Hell forever.

It was Mrs. Littell, or "Mama" as we called her, who first put the terror of God in me. She seemed to have some special arrangement with the Lord. A couple of times a year, He would strike her down. Put some sudden and mysterious affliction on her for which there was neither cause nor cure. One time a lump in her side, "big as a grapefruit," I heard her say. And she would mope around the house in longface, worry lines etched deeper than ever. Moving in slow, pained motion. Begging the Lord's forgiveness for whatever might be her sins. As much as a week or more of drawn, frowning days. Then the miracle would come. Just like that. The lump or pain or crick or whatever would disappear. And all would be right with the world again. "Thank you, Jesus," she would sing when it was all over. "God is good."

But it sure scared the Jesus out of me.

We called her Mama, Wayne and I, but she wasn't our real mom. Our real mother—the one who carried us in her womb, the one who bore the pain of us squeezing ourselves out into the world, the one who came to Mama's house to visit us on weekends—we called "Mommy." Or "my Mommy," as my brother always put it. Mama was a foster mother. A woman who "took in children." She had her own two kids, both of them girls, Margaret and Marilyn. Wayne and I and Adrian, another foster child, were just kids she took care of, who lived in her house.

It was plush and snug and comfortable, Mama's house. A womb outside of the womb. Its rooms furnished with plump upholstery like the big couch in the living room. So swollen with goosefeathers it halfways swallowed your butt when you sat in it. And almost every other chair in the house an easy chair. Every table and dresser was topped with doilies, every doily adorned with bric-a-brac. Like tiny, sepia-toned photographs in little gold-tinted tin frames. And little ceramic pixies and doodads. Or lime and cream-colored ceramic table lamps, with white, ruffle-fringed shades. All turning pee-colored with age.

A womb.

But also a little like a tomb, its windows all shrouded in heavy print-patterned drapery, the green of the vine swirling against the red of roses, cascading from ceiling to floor. And always drawn against the rudeness of the afternoon sun. The inner rooms all cast in old and dead darkness. And something darker still on the wall, a picture of a man in robes, arms and feet nailed to a cross. The first sight of blood ever to reach my eyes. Drooling down his skull. Oozing from the wound in his side.

I have had this connection ever since. Can't think of Him without also thinking of blood and pain and death. Can't think of blood and pain and death without thinking of Him. And when Chuck says "God" like that I almost flinch. For the blasphemy I have been told it is to ever take His name in vain. But then I wonder, given that chocolates and vanillas are destined to separate lots in this world, if it might be that they are bound by different sets of rules as well.

"We gotta tell the police," I say. "Gotta get them down here."

I have the pay phone in mind when I say this. The one at the gas station next to my house. Wayne and I are always back and forth to the Coke and cigarette machines there. Most often for Mrs. Knox, the blind lady who lives in one of the rooms upstairs. One of the people we share the house with, one of thirteen in all living there, everyone sharing the bathroom and kitchen. We have the two front rooms facing the street. Our mother sleeps in the living room on the pull-out couch. Wayne and I share a bed in the smaller one. We make a pretty comical pair. He's a chronic bed-wetter and I have to rock myself from side to side in order to fall off to sleep. Sometimes I wake in the night and roll over on the wet spot rocking myself back to sleep. It gives us a tangible focus for our sibling rivalry. Being the only kids in the house old enough, we are always prevailed upon to run errands for the grownups, especially Mrs. Knox, who always presses an extra "dollar fer yourself" in our hands before we go.

"Who has money?" Michael wants to know. "For the phone."

We go through the motions. Fumble through our trouser pockets. But there isn't a nickel amongst us. We trudge back across the lot. Wait again for the light. Cross Palmer. Begin to trek up toward Prospect.

A couple of summers ago we took over the crumbling tool shed in Michael's back yard, pried off the rusted hinge that held the lock, and claimed the place for a clubhouse. Next came the secret handshake. Then a secret whistle—by which, in theory at least, any one of us could summon the other two. And it has always been a given of our secret club that it is a world apart from grownups. It will not do for any of us to have our parents put in a call. This is *our* find. Our story to tell. Even if we have to tell it in person.

When we reach the police station we have to pause. Look at each other. Take in a good breath. Before we forge through the huge, forbidding doors. We find ourselves facing a giant, raised, wooden barricade, soon as we walk in. Have to tilt our heads back to see the cop sitting behind the thing. He leans forward when he sees us and grimaces. *What possible business could you kids have here?* the sour look seems to say.

Chuck and I both look at Michael and he rubs his nose. A habit of his. Running a knuckle under there. A dog's nose. Always moist and shiny. When it's clear to him there'll be no help from Chuck or me, he announces why we are here. An amazing economy of words. Four seconds tops. Textbook jargon and all.

"Hold on there, son," the cop scowls. "You found a what?"

"A pre-ma-ture em-bry-o," Michael says again, sounding out each syllable this time.

This only puts an angrier look on the cop's face.

His eyes crawl from Michael to Chuck to me.

As if he can't decide which one of us to slap first.

"A dead baby," I tell him. "In a bag. By the tracks."

"A dead baby is it?" he says. A look of fury, now, on his weathered face. But he gets on the radio and calls in a car and the next thing you know we're all rolling back down Palmer, a pair of cops in front and the three of us in the back seat. My first time ever in a police car. A bit of a disappointment too. There are no sirens, no "calling all cars," or anything like that. Not even a particular rush to get there.

We just sort of cruise down the street and park on Rockland. The cops step out of the car. A slow, *ho-hum* stretch. Fix their caps on their heads before heading down the slope. I see the flies buzzing around the bag and point. They step around me. Kind of swagger down there. Holsters dancing on their hips. Watching them, I think of John Wayne. Of men strong and hard. Of a huge, steady hand on my shoulder. Of fathers and sons.

4

My mother has a Victrola that she keeps, along with a small stash of 78-rpm records, where she supposes they are beyond our reach, on the highest of the shelves next to the fireplace. It is an ancient machine. Just like the one on the RCA record label. The one with the white dog sitting in front of it. The sound comes out of a big brass cone and you have to crank the thing to get it going. Sometimes, on holidays especially, she will climb on a chair and haul it down. And Wayne and I will fight for the coveted privilege of cranking it up. And then we will all sit there, staring into the big brass cone as music spills into the room.

The record she plays most often, the one that is foremost in my memory, is a song called *Hurt.* I can hear it now. The big, brassy crescendo that starts it off. Roy Hamilton's voice. Just as big and brassy. Leaping from the mouth of the cone.

Huuuuurt! to think that you lied to me . . .

Huuuuurt!

way deep down in-side of me . . .

You said our love was true and we'd ne-ver part . . .

Now you've some one new, and it breaks my heart . . .

Something at once soft and yet brittle enough to break at a touch gets into my mother whenever she listens to this song. Her eyes go off to some other place. And I am reminded that she is a woman. Of the sad beauty that is the woman thing in her. And I find myself wondering after my father. About him not being here. Mostly I wonder about the two of them. I wonder, with an uneasy stomach, how such a grand and sacred thing as love could ever fail to lead to happiness.

My mother tells the story of the first time she came within kissing distance of a boy. It was in high school. During gym class. They had paired up all the girls and boys for dance lessons. And my mother got partnered with a boy she didn't even know. A freckle-faced, red-haired boy. Whose face turned red too, when they had to embrace. "Red as a beet," my mother says. Always adding, "That poor child. I felt so sorry for him." The first time she said this I wondered what black devices of her young life had so battered her self-esteem that she could see her own loathsomeness in the eyes of a complete stranger.

She grew up shy to the point of pain about boys, my mother. Perhaps from living in the shadow of her sister, Lillian. Not only was Lillian fourteen years older, she seemed to have been cut from a different batch altogether. Her skin was the color of pecans. What they called "high yellah" back then. And she was built in the fashion of the times. Full and busty up top. Slender and boyish in the hips.

My mother was dark and gangly.

Lillian got all the boys.

When she was twenty-two, my mother got a job with the navy secretarial pool in Washington, DC. World War II was on at the time and they needed people. She stayed there for three and a half years. And in all that time she made no new friends and had no social life to speak of. The one exception was a party, thrown by a coworker. She allowed herself to be talked into going, but hugged the wall for most of the evening.

When she left, a young man from the party trailed her and offered to walk her home. She told him she was taking the trolley, thank you very much. But that didn't discourage him. He walked to the trolley stop and waited with her. And when the trolley showed, he hopped aboard too and sat with her and made what pleasant conversation he could. When they got to her stop and he went to step out my mother stopped him. "This is the last trolley back for the night," she told him. "I think you'd better go home."

That was the end of that.

She never saw him again.

When the war ended, so did the secretarial job. My mother moved in with her mother, Mabel. Mabel was a widow by then. Her husband Jethro had been a diabetic and died from the disease when my mother was in her teens. She was now living in Peekskill, New York, in a two-bedroom apartment near the center of town. And she had taken in three foster children from the Westchester County Department of Child Welfare in order to make ends meet. So it was three cribs in one bedroom, my mother in the other, and her mother on the pull-out couch.

One morning on her way to work—she had found a job folding and packaging goods at a nearby pajama factory—my mother noticed a young man in front of the dry cleaners next door. And she could have sworn he was checking her out. She of course gave him the "no nevermind," as she tells it. A few days later she noticed him there again. Smiling, this time.

She hurried on her way.

It played out like this a few times before my mother allowed herself "to be spoken to by him." His name was Tolan, he let her know. Tolan Stringer. He lived in Montrose, the next town over. And he worked at the cleaners, driving the delivery truck.

"And your name?" he wanted to know.

"Elizabeth," she told him, but never Liz.

My mother hates the name Liz.

After that it was, *"Hello Elizabeth,"* and *"How are you today Elizabeth?"* when he saw her. And then one day it was, *"Can I call you Betty?"* And soon after that, *"How about I come over to visit some day? After work. When your mother's home, of course."*

He had to ask more than once.

Until she finally said yes.

Mabel thought Tolan was a little young when she met him. He was just nineteen. My mother was twenty-six. And Tolan's father felt the same way from the opposite side. He was polite to my mother when Tolan brought her to meet his family—three brothers and a sister—a few weeks later. But he kept a distance. None of this got much in the way of things, though. One thing after another, the two of them fell in love. They were happy together. For a while at least.

Then my mother discovered she was pregnant.

The first thing she did was keep it to herself. The second thing she did—when it was coming to where it would be harder and harder to keep it hidden—was tell her mother. The third thing she did—her and Mabel together—was tell Tolan. The first thing he did when he got the news was tell my mother he would marry her. The second thing he did—he and my mother together—was go to the county building the very next day. To take the requisite blood test. The third thing he did was talk to his father. And the fourth thing he did, just days after he had proposed, was tell my mother he had changed his mind. He was too young, he said, to get himself married.

"*Fine*," my mother told him, "*then later for you!*"

She gave notice at the pajama factory the next week.

Despite that it had just been ordained a city, due to a robust postwar boom in light manufacturing, Peekskill remained at heart a small town. It wouldn't do for my mother to be seen with her belly out to there and no husband in sight to speak for it. Nor was abortion a consideration. It was not a thing even talked about. Not amongst any of the people my mother knew. A few weeks later she checked herself into a home for unwed mothers.

On October 6, 1948, she gave birth to my brother, Wayne Livingston Stringer. A "scrawny kid," as my mother remembers it. Who could cry "loud enough to wake the dead." And who was wailing away the next day, in fact, when Tolan showed up "out of nowhere." Just walked into the hospital room and said, "How's my girl doing?"

"What are you doing here," my mother wanted to know.

He had to come, he told her.

Had to see his son.

Wanted to do the right thing.

Sign the birth certificate.

Give Wayne his name.

My mother was surprised.

When she got out of the hospital, she stayed home with Wayne instead of going right back to her job. This enabled Mabel to earn extra cash doing day work, cooking and cleaning for another family, while my mother looked after the foster kids. And when Tolan stopped by one day with a gift for the baby, she let him. She didn't have it in her to deny him seeing his own son.

Soon he was stopping by afternoons, here and there. Always solicitous of anything my mother might want or need. Always ready to run whatever odd errand she asked of him. The extra attention must have made a difference. Because despite how hurt and disappointed my mother had been with him, a month or so later she and Tolan were dating again. And despite that my mother never got much out of "fooling around," as she puts it, one thing after another, a few months later she ended up pregnant all over again.

Then Mabel died. Dropped dead of a heart attack in the middle of cleaning someone else's house. My mother was home when she got the call. In the kitchen. Preparing baby formula. The phone rang. She picked it up. And the lady on the other end, the person for whom her mother worked, told her Mabel had suddenly collapsed. Just like that. Fine one minute and then, *Boom*. They had called an ambulance, but she was pronounced dead at the scene. My mother hung up. Called her sister Lillian in Harrison, who came to Peekskill the next day.

Two days after that Mabel was put in the ground.

There was now nothing to keep my mother in Peekskill. Nothing for her but more of Tolan if she stayed. And nothing with him, since it seemed that she couldn't resist him, but having more babies. She called the county. Told them to come pick up their foster kids. And when the county social worker assessed her situation she suggested she take Wayne with her too. Put him up for adoption. My mother said no. Wayne was her son. She would never think of giving him away. The lady argued that given my mother's plans to leave and that she'd have no means of support or home of her own, it might be best. But my mother simply refused. In the end they settled on a temporary foster home for him. Just until my mother could get back on her feet and take him back. So Wayne was taken to the Bronx. To the home of Mrs. Daisy Littell.

I came into the picture a little over a year after my brother. On October 24, 1949. I wasn't alone either. I had a twin sister. Only she didn't make it. She died five hours after she was born. The surgeon heading the delivery team was a kind and gentle soul. A Dr. Caverly. My mother was so taken by his bedside manner, that when it came to a first name for me she borrowed his. I thus became Caverly Eden Stringer.

There was no visit from my father this time. My mother had had enough of him. She had put him out of her life once and for all. Which meant, in the long run, that he was out of Wayne's life and out of mine too.

5

When the cops get to the plastic bag they come to a stop.

"Jesus, Joseph and Mary," I hear one of them mutter.

The other one turns and vomits on the grass.

I wanted sirens and now here they come. A second patrol car, screaming up the block. Two cops hustle out and go down the slope. An ambulance follows. And a pair of medics go down the slope. Six people, now, around the bag. You can't even see the dead baby anymore for all the guys with badges down there. They huddle and point. Point up at us. Point down at the little body. Point to each other. They search. Snoop around under the bridge. Pick up a ditched whisky bottle. A few fresh cigarette butts.

Then, everyone back up the slope, where by now a cluster of residents has gathered, drawn by all the goings-on. A pair of police barricades are set up. A rope stretched between them. The crowd nudged back behind it. A white sedan pulls up and a woman gets out. She has a no-nonsense look on her face. Her hair is gathered back from her skull. She strides over to a cop and flashes her ID.

"*Daily Times*," I hear her tell him.

Chuck's eyes are all over the place. Michael's are down the hill. Frozen there. His hands are in his pockets. He is very still. I turn and watch the cop and the reporter. Both talking. Both gesturing. He scribbling in his notebook. She scribbling in hers.

The pointing begins again. Here. There. Back at us.

"Those three, there?" I hear the lady say.

Her pen is aimed at us when she says it. I nod *yes* as she walks over to us. An altogether loud nod. One that begs *Talk to me! Put me in your paper!*

She puts up a smile.

Takes the three of us in with a sweep of her green eyes.

Tells us she is from "the paper."

"May I ask you a few questions?" she says.

I see Michael go to speak. See him take in a breath.

"I'm the one who found it," I say. Before he has a chance to get his erudite gab into play.

The reporter turns to me, pen poised.

Wants to know my name.

Wants to know how you spell *Caverly*.

Wants me to tell her what happened.

I tell her the story. But I am strangely disconnected when I do. It is all of a sudden too hot to touch as a real thing, if that makes any sense. I think of the three of us, Michael, Chuck and me, of the secret club that we are. And hear myself telling the woman how we had "got word that a premature embryo was in the area and decided to investigate." I tell her about kicking the bag. That I knew not to touch the thing with my hands "in case of fingerprints." I tell her about deciding right away to go to the police. That we knew it was a "case for the cops."

I tell her all this and it isn't me talking. It's Sam Spade, private eye, spinning the words. And who watches yet another car arrive. An official-looking wagon. *Westchester County Board of Health* is stamped on the side. Another woman, a blonde with her hair in ringlets, gets out and shows her ID. It's Sam Spade who sees the police lift the rope for her and walk her down the hill. Who watches her step around the little corpse. Look at the thing first this way and then that. Pull out a camera. Begin snapping pictures. Then wiggle into a pair of rubber gloves. Pick up the tiny corpse like it was a roast chicken. And drop it into a plastic bag. But it is Caverly Stringer who wonders, then, whose mother she might be. What that could possibly be like.

My brother was seven and I was still six when our mother came to get us. It must have been a weekend because weekends were for her visits. And Mama Littell had got Wayne and me presentation-ready and sat us in the parlor to await the *ding dong* of the bell. It was a bright room, the parlor. Thanks to the bank of lace-curtained windows along one wall. The brightest room in the house. When she arrived, my mother greeted us on one knee. Gathered us in against her coat and told us, as we bent to kiss her cheek, that she had "good news."

I didn't know if she meant kid-good or grownup-good. Grownup-good often being unfathomable to me. We were going home, she told us. She had found a place for us to live. And I thought *kid-good, maybe.* I'd be out of the way, at least, of Mama's dark dealings with the Lord. But my mother had not just found a place for us to live. Somewhere in there she had found religion too. Just woke up early one Sunday, as she tells it. Glimpsed out the window. At the bright spring morning outside. And saw the hand of God in it. She got up then and there and went to church. Has been a regular churchgoer ever since. Which made it a given that Wayne and I were expected to go regularly too. Not just to Sunday School either, like we had done in the Bronx. But to real church. The fire and brimstone, foot-stomping, hand-clapping, speaking in tongues kind of services the grownups went to.

Wayne seemed to take to this right away. Almost soon as he could utter the Lord's Prayer. I didn't. Didn't like church. All that murk and gloom inside. The thought of a ghost stalking the place, no matter how holy, a frightening thing. I didn't like preachers. Didn't like the sweat of their tarry brows. Or that snowy white handkerchief that dabbed it away. That always struck me as obscene somehow. I didn't dislike church people, really. Just that, lost, broken and resigned as they were, I found them too heartbreaking to face.

Most of all I hated the trek through "the flats" each Sunday. The suffering four-story walkups along the avenue. Wedged shoulder to shoulder. The fading frame houses on the side streets. Squeezed in with cinderblock warehouses and blonde brick factories. The ruined sidewalks and leaning lampposts. The liquor store. Pool hall. Bar. None of which bothered to put on a respectable face. Like their counterparts up the street. All of this standing in blunt testimony to the stingier birthright of those unlucky enough not to have been born vanilla.

The Department of Health station wagon, I notice, is less than white. There is a film of grime encroaching at the edges. Seeing this panics me as it drives off, dead baby inside. I don't know why.

Then, the cops. Shooing people away from the scene.

"Show's over," one of them says. "Let's take it home."

He halts Michael, Chuck and me, though, when we turn to leave. Takes down our names and addresses before letting us go. "And listen," he tells us. Putting up a serious regard. "I wunnett say a word about this to anyone. Till we get this sorted out. Okay? 'Sfor yer own safety, unnerstan?"

I understand.

Whisky. Cigarettes. Death.

"And I mean *anyone,*" he adds.

We walk home. The quietest walk ever amongst us. No mind for cracks and small stones now. Chuck peels off first. Continues up Rockland when we cross Palmer. He lives in the Rockland Arms Apartments just off the corner. It will be many years from now before I learn that, vanilla or no, his house was on the welfare man's rounds, the same as mine.

6

I do just as the cops say. I say nothing, not even to my mother, when I walk in the door. I sit on the living room couch. Try to stare my thoughts down by watching cartoons on TV. At dinner I can only put down a few forks full before I have to push my plate away.

"Are you all right?" my mother asks, and I can see the alarm in her eyes. Food is a sacred thing with her. Just come to the table late and you touch a nerve. Not eating your food is practically a sin. I tell her I'm okay. Just that I am not hungry. That maybe I'll eat something later. That me and the guys had had some candy earlier and it spoiled my appetite. Just as I am telling her this, I catch the picture of Him out of the corner of my eye. Bearing down from the mantel. His ubiquitous eyes observing how effortless it has become for me to feed my mother lies.

When I was eight years old I was fooling around underneath my bed one Saturday afternoon. Navigating around the boxes and cartons under there, pretending I was trawling the ocean floor for lost treasures, I came across my mother's Sterno stove. A little, black, tin box. With slotted holes in the top. And a can of grease inside. And it got into me to fire it up.

I've seen my mother use the thing to heat up the hot comb she straightens her hair with Saturday nights, getting ready for church the next day. Having straight hair is a big thing among the grownups in my house. Hubert, the guy who lives in one of the rooms upstairs, puts this smelly, poison stuff in his to straighten it out. And walks around with a rag wrapped around his head all the time. With him it's for Friday night, though. When he goes out on the prowl for women.

Jackie, the woman who lives down the hall, heats her hot comb on the stove in the kitchen when she does her daughter Charlotte's hair. We all call her Cookie instead of Charlotte. Because she's so cute. And I know she doesn't like having this done very much. Her *ouch!* has more anger than pain in it when the comb burns her scalp.

Then there's Tootsie, who has one of the rooms on the second floor. She's on the young side. In her twenties perhaps. But an adult to me all the same. Very pretty too. Secondhand though my notions about such things may be. High yellow skin. And long, chestnut-colored hair that cascades in graceful arcs to her shoulders. One Friday night I caught her through the open bathroom door. Leaning over the sink with an eyebrow pencil. Trying to draw a false mole on her cheek just under her right eye. And have wondered about the mysterious ways of women ever since.

I have never seen her wield a hot comb though. Even though her hair is always straight. And she is forever going on about her cousin who, she says, had been lucky enough to be born with "good hair." Which, if you turn it around, implies that those of us not so lucky must have "bad hair." And frankly, when they put it like that—good hair versus bad—you can't help getting the idea, particularly considering the fuss my mother makes straightening hers for church, that there must be some connection between the straightness or kinkiness of one's hair and one's nearness to God.

So there I was. Under the bed with the lit Sterno stove. I didn't burn the thing very long. Just a minute or so. I didn't want to set the whole bed on fire. I just wanted to see the flame lick up through the grill. But when I put the lid back on the can to douse the thing it started gushing smoke. And my mother, who was in the next room going at the rug with a broom, stuck her nose in the door wanting to know what was burning.

"Burning?" I heard myself say.

I was amazed how perfectly alarmed I managed to sound. It had been a lazy afternoon. Wayne was off somewhere else. I was enjoying having the room to myself, by myself. The last thing I needed was to get my mother going.

"Nothing's burning," I said.

I hadn't ever lied to my mother before. Not that I could remember. Lying, she had made clear to Wayne and me, was among the surest ways to tick God off and earn yourself a berth in hell. Yet this one had come out as natural as can be. Just rolled off my lips. And when my mother persisted, wanting to know *where*, if nothing was burning, *was all the smoke coming from*, I suggested, without batting a lash, that it was perhaps not smoke at all but simply the dust she had raised with her broom.

My mother isn't stupid. She certainly knows smoke from dust. But she never said anything. She roused me from under the bed. Shooed me out of the room. Got me busy doing something "useful," as I remember. Which meant putting me to work helping with the house chores. But she never called me on the lie. Which only left me to wait with barely subsumed terror upon a wrath far mightier than hers. To spend a few nights eyes-to-the-ceiling pondering the grapefruit in Mama's side. Whether it was a painful thing. To think of cancer and disfigurement. To imagine all sorts of tragic horrors I had heard whispered from grownup lips.

The fact that none of these things happened, that God declined to extract any penance for my sin, didn't put me at ease. It only raised the stakes. Only left the matter between my mother and me. And one lie leading to the next, each lie steepening my sense of doom, I began to feel like an intruder even at home. A devil in my mother and brother's midst. And sometimes—and this is not an easy thing to tell you—I would wish for nothing else but that one of them would fall from grace.

About a year after the thing with the Sterno stove, the thing with Victor happened. Victor was big and scary. A mean-eyed boy. A prepubescent thug in biker's rags, really. To whom the art of intimidation seemed to be second nature. Wayne and I first laid eyes on him a year or two back. We were on our way home from the school playground one evening. Had just turned on to Rockland. When Victor and a crony of his cut us off. They came skidding up on bikes. We didn't wait around to see what they had in mind. We flew back up Rockland. Back toward the school grounds. And they lit out after us. And finally cornered us in a little alcove of sorts in the back of Central School. I was sure we were about to get the living daylights kicked out of us. If for no other sake than spite. But Victor had something else in mind.

"Okay, take 'em out," he croaked. He and his partner straddling their bikes. He uncocked a cruel, stubby finger, and gestured toward our crotches. "Lemme see 'em."

I couldn't believe what I was hearing. Nothing I had ever heard about Victor implied that he might be that way. Not that I actually knew anything specific about being that way at the time. I looked at Wayne. He was spook-eyed as only Wayne could be. Like he had just got a glimpse of the devil himself. And that in itself was frightening. He was, after all, my older brother. My hope was he would have an idea what to do. Say something, at least.

Instead, he reached for his fly. And I followed suit. We stood there, exposed before the mute scrutiny of our two captors, for what seemed like a long time. Me thinking, but trying not to think about, what consequences might be in store for us if one of them pulled out a knife.

Then Victor said, "Jiggle 'em. Get 'em hard."

For a second I just looked at him. It had never before been suggested to me that the thing could do that. Although on some instinctive plane—the same instinct that was now beginning to transmit vague terrors about molestation—it just as quickly made sense that it should. I jiggled away, curious as well as frightened. But with my eyes gazing off into the distance all the while. Refusing to bear witness. And finally shrugged. Disappointed and humiliated at the same time. Whatever the mechanism that should have caused the expected transformation, it never kicked in.

Victor and his sidekick exchanged a smirky glance. Abruptly popped their butts back on their bikes. And sped off out of the school yard. Leaving Wayne and me blinking into the gathering dusk with our dicks in our hands. We stared at our pant cuffs all the way home. And never made mention between ourselves of exactly what had happened. In the end I simply wrote it all off as part of Victor's dark weirdness and resolved to steer as well clear of him as possible.

But walking down Rockland Avenue one Saturday, I heard someone call out. And when I peered over my shoulder I saw Victor. He was on foot this time. About twenty yards behind me. Coming up on me double-time. I saw the leer on his florid face and raced for home. I shot down Rockland. I can run when I want to. Cut left on Palmer. Bolted up the stairs to my house. Careened through the front door and slammed it shut.

My mother must have heard the ruckus.

She called out through the door of our two rooms.

"It's just me," I said.

I scrambled into the kitchen. The window there was too high for me. I pulled up a chair and stood on it. Leaned on the sink and peered out. There was Victor rounding the corner. At full stride.

I heard the hallway door open.

"Caverly?" my mother said again.

"Yes," was all I said. This was a kid thing after all. Bringing grownups into it would only make an all the more messy business of it.

Then the doorbell rang.

I heard my mother go down the hall.

"Wait . . ." I said.

I heard her open the door . . .

Heard her say, "Yes? . . ."

Heard Victor's lumbering voice . . .

I couldn't make out what he was saying. Only noticed the chirpy tone. He was obviously trying to worm his way in the door by passing himself off as a friend. My mother is a humble woman. She has nothing but deference for our neighbors. Any minute now, knowing her, Victor would be *inside the house*!

I stepped down from the chair. There was always the back door. I could go through the back yard. Over to Michael's house. Pound on his door. I began to make for the kitchen door. Then froze. Dumbstruck. To hear my mother say, smooth and sweet as Victor had been,

"I'm sorry. Caverly isn't home right now."

A moment of silence followed.

But Victor didn't let it go at that. He tried petitioning for a glass of water. He tried asking himself in to wait for me. Yet my mother was resolute in fending him off.

I heard him say, "Well" and then "Okay."

I heard the door go shut.

And my mother's footsteps down the hall.

She came into the kitchen and looked at me. A *well, are you going to tell me about it?* look on her face. I could only gape at her. Unable to swallow that she had just stood there and lied for me.

A minute later there would be much worse stuff to swallow down. A picture of my mother writhing in Hell, for one. The flames licking around her fading apron. And the hard, ugly fact that I had wished it all, for another. A minute later the wall of her holiness, more wide than tall, would once again put a great divide between us. But right then all I wanted to but did not do—it being that we had outgrown the habit—if indeed we ever did have it—was to hug my mother. Throw my arms around her waist. Bury my nose in her apron. Savor that for this one quick interval at least she was not just mother, not just God's mistress, not just matriarch of his hard standard, but flesh and blood.

7

The next morning. Working my way through breakfast. My mother, Wayne and I sitting around the foldaway table in the living room. I stumble across a thought that is so unsettling I have to get up and out of the house. It haunts me as I walk next door to see what Michael's up to. I find him still in his robe when he opens the door. And his eyes are dark and hollow. His mother is not there. She has the early shift at the phone company.

"You just getting up?"

"I had a nightmare last night," he tells me. Not answering the question. Just peering at me. As if he'd just noticed me standing there. "I dreamt that lady came back. The one who took the baby. There was a knock on the door and when I opened it she was standing there. She had that . . . bag with her. And she said, 'You can have this back now. We're all through with this,' and handed it to me."

He tells me this gazing off at some distant thing. Then goes silent. I had come to unload my own unwelcome thoughts on him. To have him disperse them with his clean, worldly words. But I don't. I see that, calm as he had seemed on the scene yesterday, the whole thing shook him as much as it did me. So I keep my dark thoughts to myself. I don't dare give them any more life than they already have. We sit there on Michael's little square of a porch. Not saying anything for a good while. Until there is no other idea in my head but to go back home.

My mother is doing laundry when I get there. She has this little General Electric canister washing machine that she hauls from the closet to do our clothes in. I don't remember the thing ever working quite right. She has to sit on the lid, once she starts it up, to keep it from dancing around the room.

"Are you all right?" she wants to know. It being summer and me being in the house in the middle of the day.

I tell her I'm fine. That it's just that nobody's around. The lie rolls off my tongue. I turn on the TV. Look for something to watch. But it is hard to hear above the steady *chug chug chug* of the washing machine. We are sitting like this, me way forward on the couch, trying to hear the TV. And my mother riding her washing machine. When a squeal rings out from above. And Tootsie comes flying down the stairs. Her hair bundled up in a towel. She looks Egyptian.

"Betty!" she says, at our door. "Did you see this?" She waves a copy of the *Daily Times* at us. "Your son is in the paper! Look!"

My mother takes it from her and her eyes go wide.

". . . Oh my God," she says as she reads the thing. "Oh dear Jesus in Heaven!"

As I am given to understand things, my mother's references to Him are above blasphemy. She's a Christian. She's been baptized. She's "in the church," as they put it.

"That explains why you weren't hungry last night," she says, setting the paper down. "I thought you were coming down with something."

I snatch the paper up. Speedread the thing. Find my name in the second paragraph. None of my Sam Spade story is there. Nothing about our "investigation." Just the facts. That the police are looking into the origins of a newly born "fetus" discarded under the Rockland Avenue bridge. And discovered by three Mamaroneck boys. The only direct quote from me is *"We knew we should call the police."*

The fuss draws my brother from the back room. He spends a lot of time in there. He has scrapbooks. A whole bunch of them. In them he keeps the minutiae of his life. Bits of paper. Pieces of cloth. The winning ticket stub from the night we saw Jackie Robinson. Clippings of people and things that catch his odd fancy. And file cards too. One for every single thing he owns.

"How come you didn't tell me about this?" my mother says.

I point with my chin at the newspaper. Wayne walks over. Picks it up. Makes his face a blank before he starts to read.

"You did the right thing," Tootsie tells me. "You don't know who could be involved. Could be one of the neighbors. You never know. You know what they say. Even a fish wouldn't get in trouble if it kept its mouth shut. You're a smart kid."

I don't let on that I had only done what the police had told me to do. I like being called smart. It is at the top of the very short list of things that are good about me. Wayne says nothing when he puts the paper back down. Just sucks a quick blast of air in through his nose and fingers his glasses back against his brow. When he wants, my brother can be a stone. Won't reveal a single blessed thing. It's the one undeniable power he has over me. Leaving me wanting like that.

"How about that," Tootsie tells my mother. "Your son's a hero! You should be proud of him."

I like the sound of that too.

I like even more that my mother allows herself a quick smile at this. It is a rare thing, my mother's smile. And the half frown she often wears on her face seldom fails to wound me somehow. "*Can't go around smiling like an idiot all the time*," she bristles whenever I bring the matter up. And I'll be left feeling too selfish by half. Still, it is a thing I ever yearn for from her. A simple smile. A sign that, yes, despite everything, there can be happiness.

At bedtime Wayne rolls right off. It's one of his silent nights. When he lays there until sleep comes without so much as a wayward peep, I know better than to ask. Whatever is eating him, he'll never give me so much as a hint what it is. But I think I know anyway. Yesterday, when I left to join Chuck and Michael, I was very sly about getting out of the house without giving him a chance to ask if he could come along. He had asked, in fact, what I was planning to do that day and I had told him nothing much. The problem is Wayne, skinny as he is, is forever breaking himself. Like the time we were rummaging through the piles of lumber in Michael's back yard and he fell and caught his arm on a five-inch nail. It went right through. Or when he fell off the swing at the school playground and fractured his wrist. Just like that. With him, it is scary doctor stuff instead of fun. So I lied to him. Told him nothing much.

Who knew we were going to end up with our names in the paper?

So it's the silent treatment from him. And me staring into the dark of the room. Too keyed up to go to sleep. Thinking *People will read the paper. They will see my name. I'll become someone who matters. I will at last be . . . visible.* A big thing to me, being visible. I even imagine that finding that baby will somehow set everything right. That I might not have to be sent away. That perhaps they might forgive the thing with the boot and I will be let back in school in the fall.

But as the flatness of fall supplants the bluster of summer, death in a brown paper bag by the tracks being its last hurrah, nothing in the scheme of things really changes. It still feels very much like *me* and *them.* And I am never able to entirely shake the thing I have kept to myself. The unnerving thought I couldn't bring myself to share with Michael or anyone else. That if a just-born child could be beyond God's protection, what could possibly stand between every dark, evil, bloody terror imaginable and a far less pure soul like me?

8

We're all in the auditorium when it happens. Halfway through the Spring Pageant. Only you wouldn't know it's spring to look outside. There's still snow on the ground. And it's been drizzling off and on since morning too. So it was boots and raincoats and a slushy mess coming in to school. It's springtime up on the stage, though. The hot white glow of spotlights standing in for sunshine. And bright, hand-painted lilacs and magnolia blossoms all over the place.

The squirmy thing about assembly is facing all the teachers I have had at once. Knowing I have bad history with them all. All except Mr. Johnson that is, whom I had last year for fifth grade. His first year here and they put me in his class. It was different having someone who looked like me up there in front of the room for once. I felt a lot less like an outsider. Still and all I was distressed with Mr. Johnson half the time. Refusing to treat me any differently than the rest of his students. Which I entirely expected he would. I guess I got him confused with the father thing, both of us being the same color and all. And I guess I spent so much energy trying to put myself across as a worthy son that I didn't have any left for causing trouble.

I'm sitting twelve rows back. With the rest of the sixth-graders. It's two rows to a grade. Starting with the first-graders up front, then working back from there. I have Mr. Nagle this year. And things have not gone smoothly with him. I wasn't in his class more than a month before I got into it with the guy at the desk next to mine. A "tall drink of water," as my mother would say, named Joe. I was cutting out my moon—we were all making cards for Halloween—when Joe reached across my desk, stuck the tip of his finger between the blades of my scissors—a pair of those dumb, snub-nosed things they give you in school—and told me "Cut my finger."

Just like that.

Joe's kind of a jerk, if you want to know the truth.

One of those guys who takes an hour and a half to get through a paragraph when it's his turn to read out loud in class. I should have ignored his whole bother. But he was so determined about the whole thing. "Go 'head," he kept saying. "Do it. Cut my finger." Daring me to do it. So I went ahead and did it. Gave his finger a little snip. Just enough to raise a small gob of blood. Next thing you know he's screaming bloody murder. Running around the room. Yelling "HE CUT MY FINGER! STRINGER CUT MY FINGER!" Like he hadn't practically begged me to do it.

The surprise was how Mr. Nagle handled the whole thing. He didn't get on me in front of the class, which I really hate. He took me into the hallway to talk with me. And even then he didn't tear me down. Just told me I knew better than to take Joe up on a dare. That I was smarter than that. That between me and him, Joe could be a problem sometimes. Then he had me switch seats with a guy up front so Joe would be "out of my hair."

So *he* would be out of *my* hair.

Then he did something none of my teachers have done except to hold me back. He put a hand on my shoulder. That really got to me. I mean you'd expect him to be on Joe's side. It was a pretty crummy thing to do after all. Me cutting his finger like that. But that's the thing about Mr. Nagle. He always seems to be on my side too. Even though I keep messing up. And each time I do I could just kick myself. Because, I swear to God, the last thing I want is to make him give up on me.

The third-graders have just finished their bit. So we're looking at an empty stage. Mrs. DeRay—perfect name for a music teacher if you ask me—rises from her piano bench. Gives a nod to the wings. The fourth-graders file out. Moving stiff as robots. I hear smothered snickering as they gather in the center of the stage. All of them looking like something out of a nightmare. The pinkness peeking out from the edges of the blackface makeup they are wearing inflates their eyes and mouths to grotesque proportions.

My eyes go to the little girl in the middle. Huge, wide, blue eyes. Auburn hair, done up in pigtails. Every feature as trim and perfect as her button-down blouse. *What an awful thing has been done to her,* I'm thinking. *Smearing her cute little moon face with black like that.* I also think of my sister. Who never made it beyond the incubator. I don't know why she pops into my mind. I only know that it's something I don't like to think about.

There's always a skit. To set up the song they are going to sing. And they go right into it. A skit about slaves from the look of it. Really hamming it up. *Youall*-ing this. *Honeychile'*-ing that. Making two syllables of every *hey-re* and *they-re.* My eyes drop to the floor. Don't want to catch anyone peeking back my way. *No comparisons today, thank you very much.* And from this vantage point—hearing but not seeing—they begin to sound riotously surreal. Just for fun I start doing it too in my head. Start talking with a drawl.

I carry on like this with my brother sometimes. Especially when he gets all quiet and moody and to-himself like he does. And I have to get him laughing to make it halfways feel like we're brothers. He has a kind of funny sense of humor. Funny strange, I mean. It only clicks in on the weirdest things. We'll be watching a Western on TV, for instance. And every time someone gets his head bashed in with a tomahawk Wayne will go into conniptions. Like I said, weird. You never know what will make him laugh. I can usually get him, though, with a funny voice. I've gotten pretty good at picking them up.

I pull my eyes from the floor long enough to take a quick glimpse around for him. He's in Mrs. Chapman's class. The other sixth-grade teacher. He should be done with elementary school altogether and on to junior high. But he was out for a few weeks last year. When he fractured his arm falling off the playground swings. And he was never able to catch back up with the rest of the class. So he got left back. He doesn't have an easy time of it in school, to tell the truth. The problem is he never speaks up for himself. He's so busy being quiet and polite you'd never know it from him what he does or doesn't get.

Wayne's hot with music, though. He gets that right away. It's a gift he has. He's had it since when we were back in Mama's house. We were sitting in her parlor one afternoon. Perry Como's lazy baritone crooning from the radio in the other room. When Wayne got up. Walked straight over to Mama's upright piano in the corner of the room. Flipped the cover up. And started tapping out the melody. He didn't miss one note. Then Mama running into the room. Hugging Wayne. Carrying on about what a talented child he was.

"My God," she said, "you have a gift!"

I hated him for the rest of the day.

In school it's me who gets it right away. I get squirmy when you make too fine a point of something. My mind starts to look for something to chew on. I'll start making puns in my head, for instance. Out of what the teacher is saying. Puns that, sooner or later find their way to my lips. And, one thing after another, I end up getting myself in a jam.

I'm looking at the guy next to me. A kid named Dana. I don't know him except to see him around. Funny thing is, even though I don't know him, for some reason I wish he were my brother. I have no idea why. I'm looking at him because there's a big fat grin on his face. And he's snickering away under his breath. Snickering because I'm doing it out loud now. Not too loud. Just enough for him to hear.

"Mah, mah, mah, honey chile'," I'm saying. Shaking my head from side to side. Like I've seen the servants do in *Gone with the Wind.* "But you sho' does looks a sight!"

The guy to my right starts snorting over this too.

But Dana's laughter is the bigger prize.

The beginning of a bond in my eyes.

"Well Ah do duck lair," I go on. A little louder now. "But it sho' is a mostus fine day, Miz Charlotte."

Snicker. Chortle. Snort.

There are two shows going on now.

One on stage and the other twelve rows back.

Then I hear, "Would you be quiet, Stringer!"

. . . Someone hissing this at me.

. . . Snapping my name like the crack of a whip.

. . . Billy Brauninger. Paleface, freckle-cheeked Brauninger. Twisted around in his seat. An all-too-adult reproach curling his purplish upper lip.

"Some of us are trying to watch the show," he says.

Brauninger—no one ever calls him Billy, it's always Brauninger—has that bookworm thing going. You know, turtleneck, corduroys and penny loafers. Doesn't like sports. Ducks gym all the time. Kisses up to the teachers. Most of the kids don't have much use for him. But as they have even less use for me, when he says *some of us are trying to watch the show* the "us" of it halfways sticks.

I give him my mean face. Snap his name right back.

"Shadddup Bra-a-a-au-nin-ger," I tell him.

He rolls his eyes to the ceiling. But he wiggles back around in his seat. Shakes his pink head from side to side before he does. Puts his nose up in the air. And gives me that look I hate. The *whatever are we to do with you* kind of look my teachers condemn me with when I act up. Wayne too. He and Brauninger suffer from the same thing, I guess. Both wanting to be grownups instead of kids. The kid thing not working all that well for either of them.

They made Wayne a hall monitor once. Before he fractured his arm last year. Probably because he's so well behaved. And whenever he got into those white gloves and put that white sash across his chest he became a force to be reckoned with. He'd get that no-nonsense look on his face. His bottom lip turned all out. Like our mother gets when she wants you to know she isn't playing. And he'd stand on the landing just waiting on the poor sucker who'd make the slightest wrong move. No matter who you were. Big or small. Stray out of the line—or, God forbid, run—on the stairwell and Wayne would be on you like white on rice. I'd practically tiptoe past him myself. There was no way I'd ever give him the satisfaction of jumping down my throat in front of the whole school. Besides which, I kind of got a kick out of his stalwart tyranny, if you want to know the truth. Wayne up there on the landing. Making them all toe the line.

With Brauninger and me, though, it's another thing altogether. A matter of principle. An article of the grade-schooler's unspoken code. That I be clear and demonstrative in disdaining a teacher's pet like him and all that he stands for.

I go right back to carrying on.

Not even looking at Brauninger.

As if he doesn't matter in the least.

But then when I do take a quick peek—to hammer the nail home by lording it over him—he's not there.

He's . . . down at the end of the aisle.

. . . Right at Mr. Nagle's shoulder.

. . . And he's pointing back at me.

Just as Mr. Nagle turns to look I yank my eyes away. Put them up on the stage. Try to act as if I'm hanging on every utterance out of the fourth-graders' mouths. But a second later Mr. Nagle is bent at my side. Giving me one of his looks. Not an angry or exasperated look. But level and unassuming. Patient even. A look in which I nonetheless always see an uglier me reflected. Since it only ever comes to his face when I've messed up.

"What's the problem here?" he says.

Up front Mrs. DeRay is standing again.

She sounds a note on her pitch pipe.

The fourth-graders go "*H-m-m-m-m*" back.

"Nothing," I tell Mr. Nagle. "No Problem."

"*. . . Ca-r-e-e-e me b-a-a-ck to o-o-o-ld Vir-gin-ee,*" the fourth-graders begin to sing. A song straight out of the songbook Mrs. DeRay always brings with her when she comes around with her autoharp for music period.

"*. . . The-e-res where the cot-ton and the corn and 'ta-ters grow.*"

Mr. Nagle peers over his shoulder. Regards the action on stage for a silent second. He takes in a breath when he turns back. There's a hint of a grimace on his face. His eyes drop down.

"Look. This thing's almost over," he says. More to his watch than to me. "Am I going to have to come back here again?"

I tell him "No." And even though I can't quite look at him when I say it I really mean it.

He goes back to his seat.

I quit horsing around.

Just gape at the fourth-graders.

. . . There's *where I labored so hard for ole' massa.*

Day after day in the field of yell-ah corn.

The first time I was obliged to join my classmates in singing this song I had to ask Mrs. DeRay what *massa* meant. She had to shush the class before she could tell me for all the snickering that erupted. Then she did her halting best to explain the whole thing to me. That slaves were once called *darkies.* That *darkies* called the people who owned them *master.* And that it came out *massa* the way they said it. Then *she* had to shush the class all over again. I was sorry I brought the whole thing up. I haven't been able to listen to that song since without thinking about darkies. Another thing I don't much like thinking about.

I drop my eyes from the stage. And when I do there's Brauninger. Still wrenched around in his seat. Not so interested in the show any more, apparently. I resolve to just stare him down. To stone into submission with cold contempt the malicious glee I expect to see in his eyes. What I'm not prepared for, however, what proves to be beyond the tolerance of some blind, seething thing in me, is the smug, satisfied, feline glimmer I find in them instead.

I fly out of my seat.

Lunge—over two rows of folding chairs—straight for him.

But Brauninger's more athletic than he has ever let on. When I careen into his chair he is no longer there. He's already elbowing his way out of the aisle. Heading for the exit. I light out after him, not caring for the toes I am crushing.

"Caverly? . . ." I hear Mr. Nagle call.

His voice fades behind me.

Brauninger scrambles into the hallway. And cuts a quick right through an open door. I bounce off the jamb making the turn. But quickly recover. Oblivious to the shock to my shoulder. Oblivious to everything except getting my hands on the little snitch. He ducks behind the curtains in the rear of the stage and I chase his heels. A roar of laughter swells up from the audience. The two of us a pair of amorphous humps in the backdrop as the pageant plows towards its dismal finale. We pile out of the opposite door. Me mere inches from him now. Close enough to snatch at his shirt collar and bring him down. But a couple of teachers are waiting for us in the corridor. Brauninger ducks behind them. I have no choice but to skid to a stop. There is that look on their faces that I have drawn all too often. Part pity. Part exasperation. Part . . . something else. *Disappointment*, I decide, glimpsing Mr. Nagle down the hall.

I spend what is left of the afternoon sitting across from Mr. Gingrich's desk. Roiling in my own discontented stew. He hands me a note while I'm there. For my mother, he says. The envelope is sealed. But I know the drill. She will have to come to school with me and meet with him.

When the three o'clock bell sounds I shoot up the stairs. Retrieve my coat from the hooks along the corridor and put it on with one eye trained on Mr. Nagle's classroom door. One by one the kids trickle out.

But no sign of Brauninger. I gather my boots and turn into the doorway to show myself. And I realize that this is all I want to do really. That it will be enough for me to know that Brauninger will slink home in terror, peeking over his shoulder all the way.

But then Mr. Nagle steps into the doorway. Arms folded across his chest. Looking bigger and more formidable than ever. A wall between me and Brauninger. He would of course do this. He's on the side of all us kids. And our safety is in his hands. But I can see none of this. All I can see, in the sudden, white-hot blindness singing my brain, is betrayal.

I feel my muscles go taut. Feel my fingernails dig into the squishy rubber of the boot in my hand. Feel my arm jerk suddenly upward. See the boot rocket through the air. All of this before I am even aware enough that I am doing it to have decided on a definite target. The boot slams into Mr. Nagle's face. Smacks into his left cheek so hard it ricochets off and hits the doorjamb. A look explodes on his face that I have never seen there before. It no longer even resembles the person I know. Behind him, I see Brauninger. His eyes go wide with terror. Terror not for himself anymore, but for me.

A sudden pulse of instinct tells me to run.

When Mr. Nagle lunges for me I'm already in motion. To the end of the hallway. Down the stairs. Out the front doors. Off school grounds. Down Rockland. I don't stop or look back. I do wait for the green before crossing, at the corner of Palmer and Rockland. And *squish slush* into the lot. One boot off and one boot on. And toy with the idea of tossing Mr. Gingrich's letter away. But look for flowers to pick instead. A peace offering for my mother.

When I finally go home I go straight to my room. To put my school things away, I tell my mother. I hide my one boot. Bury it way back in the closet. And see my football jersey in there. The one that Mr. Nagle gave me. Waited until three o'clock and asked to see me for a minute before I went home. Then pulled it out of the big bottom drawer of his desk. I had never worn a jersey before. I'm not a football fan. But I could tell by the weight of it in my hands that this was a good one. Certainly better than any shirt I had ever owned.

"I bought it for my son. But he doesn't like the color. He's such a picky boy," he complained. But not without a fond look in his eyes. "It's a good, sturdy shirt, though," he quickly added. "And I know *you* can use it."

I opened my mouth. Wanting to say *thank you.* Wanting to say something better than that in fact. But I felt suddenly small and ashamed. *Didn't like the color. But I knew you could use it.* A dry breaking noise gurgled up from my throat when I went to speak. And then all I wanted was to get out of there. I walked through the door and out of the building. Clutching my prize far more tightly and roughly than necessary. The thing practically burning my hands. All because Mr. Nagle just *knew* I could use it.

9

It's a Friday when the car from the county comes. A lady from child services in a Town and Country station wagon. The kind with fake mahogany panels on the side. There is a hint of a smile around her eyes when she says, "Good morning." And when I answer back she seems keen to listen. A person of good intent, it seems. Like the people at the guidance center. Where I've been going Thursdays after school since the fourth grade. Because I have "emotional problems," the school counselor said. It's on the second floor of a dingy-looking tan and gray office building across from the bus stop. But inside it's like one huge playroom. Full of toys and games and building blocks and all sorts of crayons and colored pencils and finger paints. There are tiny mom, dad, brother, and sister figures too. We were especially encouraged to play with these. They paid close attention whenever we did. Hovered over you, in fact. But mostly in a friendly, interested way.

I didn't much like the half-dozen other kids there, though. They all seemed so wound into themselves. Were all too full of sadness. Worse, they didn't seem to know how to frolic and play. It drove me to near panic seeing that. I sometimes had to take a breath before walking in the door because of this. Otherwise, I never minded much going there. It isn't all that much fun having all this anger inside. When all I really want is to fit in. To get along. To be happy. Like everybody else.

We take to the thruway. Me, hunkered down in the back seat. My back against the door. My head tilted back. Gaping up at the crisp, bright, early fall sky. At the trees flashing by. Sunlight strobing through the branches. The flora hasn't withered yet. Everything is lush and green. It's mesmerizing. Fills me with a contented sort of glee. I don't know why.

My mother is not with us. It was suggested we say our goodbyes at the curb and that I make this part of the trip alone. And in a way I'm relieved. I can hardly look at my mother these days without thinking about the thorn in her side I have become.

I came home with flowers. A fist full of dandelions. The only green thing I could find on the lot. My mother was in the kitchen. Bent over the stove in her worn apron. Its once-red roses fading into whiteness. My eyes landed on her hands, flying daintily, pinkies arched, from pot to kettle to spoon, and the letter in my pocket growing heavier. The backs of her hands are ravaged with eczema. All black and crusty from fingertip to wrist. As if they had been plunged into a deep fryer. Every night she smears them with foul-smelling salves the doctor has given her. And I suppose she prays every night for a healing miracle from the Lord. So far, neither seems to have done much good. She is forever wearing gloves, whenever she leaves the house, to cover them up.

She wore them when we went to meet with Mr. Gingrich the next day. Long, white, formal gloves. And she reached for a more formal distance when she spoke to him. Trying, with mixed results, for fancier language than she uses at home. She always does this when it is me and him and her. And I am always a little embarrassed by the pretense. I'm always a little embarrassed for Mr. Gingrich, too. His unease with us is never not in evidence. His hands constantly gravitating from this thing on his desk to that. His rump ever seeking a more comfortable spot on his seat cushion.

Half the time I wish they could do the whole thing without me. I'm hardly more than a bystander anyway. Talked about in the third person. Every now and again, when the dialogue between them reaches a lull, their eyes might wander my way and discover me sitting there. And I am ever hopeful, when they do, that this time might be the charm. That this time the two of them may have at last happened upon the thing that might fix me. But their eyes simply hover appraisingly. As if wondering how much I might fetch on the open market. Then move on.

Mr. Gingrich met us at the door. Never bothering to put up his customary twinkle eyes. His face was stern and resolved as I followed my mother into his office and found a chair. A sigh escaped him when he settled behind his desk. Drew a blue folder to him. Opened it up. A tired sigh.

"You understand things have gotten very serious," he said.

I knew right then things weren't going to end with the usual handshake and encouraging word.

"Are you okay?" the lady from Child Services says.

She is peering at me in the rear-view mirror.

I tell her, "Yeah," and her eyes stay there for a second.

"Missing your mom?" she tries.

"Just thinking," I tell her.

We have left the parkway. And are rolling through a cozy little town. Not much different from Mamaroneck. A lot more trees, though. It must be that we are close now. I straighten up in my seat. Try to imagine what the place will look like. But can't. The name alone being too fancy for any point of reference I have. But it looms ominously just ahead. Around each curve. At the crest of every rise. And an uneasy feeling begins to bubble. A feeling of forced submission. Of things beyond my choice or control coming down on me.

"You'll be all right," the lady says. Her smile in the mirror again. "There'll be lots of kids your age there. Lots of things to do. You'll see."

The notice summoning me to appear before Children's Court arrived by registered mail three weeks into August. We took the 61 bus into White Plains, my mother and I. The same bus we take when she drags Wayne and me along on one of her shopping trips, which I always dread. I hate "window shopping" especially, since it doesn't make sense to me why you would want to torture yourself ogling stuff you can't afford to buy. Wayne, though, seems to get some kind of kick out of it. He'll race ahead from store window to store window, breathless and excited, yelling "Look, Mommy, look!" and I'll have to stand there on the street cooling my heels while the two of them *ooh* and *ahh* over all the pricey goods we can never have.

The courthouse was an enormous old, gray, scary-looking building. Just like in the movies. With huge wide stairs splayed down to the street. My mother had to grunt and *Thank you Jesus* her way up them. She has had battles with her weight. And when we found our way into the courtroom, and she *Sweet Jesus*ed herself down with a plump, it struck me how much the place resembled a church. The long wooden benches. All lined up. Like pews. People sitting on them. Hands in their laps. Hushed and reverent. Everything so relentlessly up-and-up you can't help feeling small and filthy in the face of it all.

My name sounded surreal when they called me up to the bench. As if it didn't really deserve to be uttered in such a high place. I glanced at my mother. All but reached to take her hand. For what? Permission? Assurance? Consolation? I don't know. And stepped up to face the judge. An imposing man. And kindly at the same time. Snow-white hair. Watery eyes. Skin so pale and thin you could see blood vessels branching like tiny rivers through his cheeks. God and father rolled into one to me.

He gave me a friendly kind of nod just before I settled my eyes below his gaze. And, oddly, that put me at some ease. But then a man in a dark suit stepped up to a little podium. Saddled a pair of stingy, half-frame spectacles on the bridge of his nose. And in an even stingier voice, began to rattle off about *this matter* being before *that* and *pertaining to* the other. A blur of stately words. I had to stifle a giggle, it all sounded so preposterous.

He opened a folder next. And started reading from it. A blue folder. One I recognized at once. The same folder I had seen on Mr. Gingrich's desk that last time my mother and I went to see him. Despite that my teachers were forever warning me that this or that thing would end up there, I never allowed myself to believe that my "record" actually existed. Certainly nothing ever committed to ink.

But now here it was. Out loud. Echoing in the hollows of the courtroom for all to hear. A singularly one-sided, failures-only portrait of me. Screaming in anger. Kicking over desks. Snapping rulers in half. Sending books smashing against the chalkboard. On and on it went. Delivered in a clipped legalese that made it all sound so brazen and wanton, I could barely stand to hear it. And topping everything off, the final, unforgivable blow that had got me there. The thing with the boot.

Just past a swatch of houses partly obscured by maples and pines, the road narrows. We wind upward. Ascend the gentle rise of an arching one-lane blacktop slope. It snakes between a pair of red brick columns. I see a weather-worn brass plate affixed to one of them. Peer through the window as we pass. Have to squint to make out the words.

"Hawthorne Cedar Knolls School," it says.

10

First, there is intake.

A lot of running around. Being handed off from one person to the next. Filling out paperwork. Shaking hands with Mr. This and Mrs. That and Dr. So-and-So. All of them in suits. Two in glasses. One with a too-big head. They form a solicitous circle around me at one point. Asking rather than telling me what I must do.

"Would you like to set your things down there?"

"Can you tell us something about yourself?"

"Do you know why you have been sent here?"

So much attention from grownups.

It makes me self-conscious and squirmy.

. . . Next there is lunch.

The next building over. A low rectangular structure. *The dining hall,* I am told. I follow Mr. Horowitz, the guy with the too-big head, inside. A long, high-ceilinged sprawl. Segmented down its length into a series of alcoves. Each separated by a pair of perpendicular walls. I hear people eating—the *click* of plates, the *tinkle* of silverware, the low-register buzz of muted talk—more than I see them. We go over to a huge, hissing steam table. A short man with fiery and bloodshot eyes stands behind it. His dark skin and boxer's build both strain against the kitchen whites he is wearing. His eyes capture, then dismiss me.

"Nathan," Mr. Horowitz says.

"Yes, sir," Nathan says back.

He loads up a pair of plates. Slaps them down on the counter without looking up. Hamburgers and french fries I'm happy to see. And down the rail a few feet, chocolate pudding for dessert. I follow Mr.

Horowitz to the alcove just inside and to the right of the front door. I see kids my age. About fifteen of them. Seated around two long tables. Or rather two sets of three square tables butted together. They are all dressed the same. All in red, blue or yellow shorts and white t-shirts with a matching red, blue or yellow shield printed on the breasts. They are all vanilla, as my mother would say, too. Except for one kid at the far table. A short, light-skinned guy. With wavy hair instead of kinks. And not all that much of a nose to speak of.

"This is you," Mr. Horowitz says. "Cottage Five."

A ropy-muscled old guy with a bulbous, moth-eaten wad of a nose rises to greet us, one veiny cheek swelling and receding as he works on the mouthful we have caught him in the middle of. He barely stands a head taller than me. His thin lips—like the edge of two cliffs, one inverted atop the other—blanch when he swallows.

"And what 'ave we here, then?" He says in a cockney lilt that somehow perfectly fits him.

"Caverly," Mr. Horowitz says—it comes out as Cave-EARLY instead of CAV-er-lee—"this is Mr. Bedford."

Mr. Bedford puts out his hand. Smiles. Not so much with his lips but with his pale eyes. They look old and deep under the creased and drooping flesh of his brows.

"Mr. Bedford is the cottage father," Mr. Horowitz says.

"Call me Pop," Mr. Bedford says. Giving my hand a hearty shake.

I like the sound of that. It is not a word I have had much occasion to put to use before. I try it out under my breath as I follow Mr. Horowitz into the alcove. And like the feel of it. The *"P"*s like little explosions on my lips.

Mr. Horowitz introduces CAVE-early around at the far table when we sit down to eat. The wavy-haired kid seems friendly enough. Tells me his name is Paul. Pee Wee to his friends. Asks how I'm doing. Where I'm from. Introduces me to the kid sitting next to him. A dark-haired kid. With a roundish face. And a flat, slanting forehead.

"Charley. My best friend," he tells me.

Throws an arm up on Charley's shoulder.

Charley beams. He's nonchalant about it. Pretends to wave it all off. But the delight in his friendship with Paul is there. I can see it. Hamburgers and french fries. And now this. I'm liking it pretty good so far . . .

. . . Next, there's the tour of the cottage.

Cottage Five. That's what they call the houses here. Cottages. More like a resort than a sleepaway school. And Cottage Five is just up the slope from the entrance. By my estimate, a mere matter of seconds to be out of here on a quick trot. There are no bars. Or fences. No physical barriers of any kind to keep you in. Just the dense rash of pines that surround the place.

"Mrs. Bedford, the cottage mother," Mr. Horowitz tells me, before he knocks. The two of us across the foyer of the empty house. In front of a closed door. "She and Mr. Bedford live here. With you kids." Mrs. Bedford steps out, black hair swept up in a Jackie Kennedy coiffure. And wearing a rather smart green dress. But the hint of apple in her cheeks gives her a matronly mien. When she *hellos* us I hear a melodious Irish brogue. *All is jolly well,* it seems to convey.

We start where we are. *Living room to the right. Porch to the left.* The first, a big room. With homey touches. Plants and curtains and matched blonde wood furniture. A big console TV stands against one wall. The porch is a narrower, screened-in affair. Looking out on the field out back. A hinged ping-pong table on wheels stands folded in two against the wall. Beside it is a little table with a checkerboard top. A low, segmented apron of lacquered pinewood, extending about three feet from the wall, rings the perimeter of the room. A double-purpose concoction, I am shown. Each segment is a separate footlocker when you lift the hinged lid. And with the lids down they are benches.

We see the basement next. Where the toilets and showers are. Four of each, all in a row. And eight sinks back to back down the middle. A cloying, wet-sneaker must assaults my nose when we step inside. And a slight shudder goes through me. Such a public and impersonal place for doing private personal business.

Upstairs, though, is brighter. As we peek in rooms, I see lots of pictures. My eyes go right to them. Pictures, mostly, of cars. Full color, glossy pictures. Carefully cut from catalogs. Pictures of perfect, handsome, rich-looking dads, leaning on shiny road machines, with briar pipes tilting from their lips. Of perfect, silk-haired, town-car moms, with creamy hands that never see dishwater. Of perfectly content little boys and girls, with button noses. And eyes as round as quarters. Smiling from the back seats of station wagons, parked on driveways smooth as glass. In front of manicured lawns, rising up to perfect homes. Pictures of a perfect America, that make me ache and long one minute—there is no one in them that looks like me—and wish and dream the next.

In my room, when we get to it, it is ships. Pictures of them all over the walls. And all kinds of ship stuff arranged on the shelves. Even a life preserver. Hung on the crash bar of the emergency exit door. There are three freestanding, metal, locker-style wardrobes against the walls, each next to a bed, one of which is bare. Mrs. Bedford pulls sheets and blankets from the top of the locker next to it. Shows me how I must make my bed. Folds in the sheet and blanket tails before tucking them under.

"Hospital corners," she tells me.

Next she hauls a large package from the locker. It is wrapped in brown paper and tied with twine across its breadth and width. Almost like a gift. I see my name, "*Stringer*," scrawled across the top in bold, black magic marker.

"Thar ya' are," Mrs. Bedford sings. "Something for you."

"Me?" I say.

"I'll leave you to put your things away," she says. "I'll be right downstairs if you need anything. Just knock on the door."

When I tear into the package it is full of clothes. They are brand new. The tags still on them. A fleece-filled winter jacket on top. Gray. With a zipper front. A pair of shoes. Dark brown and round toed. Two pairs of jeans. Blue and brown. A pair of navy Farah slacks. Three print shirts. Two flannel. One polyester. Pajamas. Socks. Underwear. Everything. I arrange them on the bed. Stretch out, for a moment, next to them. *There are no windows in this room,* I notice. Just the square pane cut into the emergency door. But this makes it all the cozier to me. Only adds to the ship-like feel of things. I can picture myself lying in bed at night. Pretending I'm off on a cruise. I eyeball the new clothes. Breathe in the fresh-out-of-the-box smell. *All this and a bed all to myself again!*

11

For most of its history, Hawthorne Cedar Knolls existed as an exclusive boys' town kind of operation. Except that you had to have money or private funding to afford sending your troubled kids here. By the early sixties, though, private money began to dry up. So they decided to accept clientele referred to them and paid for by local social service agencies. Which meant exclusivity had to go, that Hawthorne had to go "public," as it were.

Only I don't know any of this. Don't know that I am among the very first of this new public wave. Or that the package of new clothes that was waiting for me is part of the deal when you're here under the auspices of the public dole. So when I dress for dinner—another surprise—and Marty eyeballs me and says, "You're *state*, huh?" I have no idea what he means.

Marty is one of my two roommates. A short, Mickey Rooney-looking guy. With a voice so dry and smoky it sounds like he has perpetual laryngitis. My other roommate, Bruce, strikes me as an odd bird. Already more grown up than the rest of us. The beginnings of a mustache dirtying his upper lip. The ship stuff is his. His father works for the Cunard lines, he is quick to let me know. A captain, he says. I meet them both when the guys get back to the house. They come in breathless and excited. Damp with sweat. I ask Marty what the matching shorts and t-shirt getup is all about.

"The Maccabeah," he says, which means nothing to me.

"We have it every year," he explains. "Three teams. Blue, red and gold. You win ribbons and stuff. Like the Olympics." Then he gives me a look. Like I'm some kind of specimen. "Where you from, anyway?" he says.

I tell him I'm from Mamaroneck. I have to say it twice.

"Mamaroneck?" he says. "Where's that? Downstate?"

"Westchester," I tell him.

"Oh," he says, one knee bent. Bouncing the toe of his sneaker on the floor. "Me, I'm from the Bronx."

"Really?" I say. "That's where I'm from. Originally."

"No shit?" he says. "The Bronx. Whereabouts?"

"East Two Hundred and Twentieth Street," I tell him. "You?"

"Grand Concourse," he says.

I've never heard of it. But grand I imagine it must be with a name like that. I picture sandy-colored high-rises. Set way back from the curb. With ivy canopies stretching out to spotless streets. Just as I'm about to ask Marty if his parents are rich, Mr. Bedford comes up the stairs. His salty voice preceding him.

"All right, lads.

"Into the shower with ya'.

"And a spit shine on your shoes.

"Get a move on now."

He sticks his head in the door.

Gives me an open-mouthed gape. Toe to head.

"You squared away there, son?" he says with a wink.

A smile crosses my lips when I nod. I can't help myself.

"Shirt collars and slacks for dinner tonight then," he tells me. "Inta' the shower with ya' first. Then chop chop."

Chop chop is right. I take the fastest shower I've ever had. I've never showered in public before. Even at Ashford Hills, the Salvation Army summer camp Wayne and I went to two summers back to back, it was one at a time. Now, here's half a dozen strangers swaggering around. One lathering up his private parts. One working a towel up the crack of his behind. Another bent over the sink. Carefully laying on the preening touch to his hair with a wet comb. All of them so casual in their nakedness.

And me suddenly at odds with my limbs.

Have my arms always been this skinny?

Have my knees always been as knobby as that?

And look at my feet! They're gigantic!

It isn't until I am in my new shoes and slacks and polyester shirt that my confidence is refreshed. When I fall out in front of the cottage with the rest of the guys and we start for the dining hall, there's a little bounce to my step. A thing that Pee Wee notices. He and Charley a pace ahead of me. Pee Wee in a white shirt and khakis and Charley in a blue dress shirt and gray slacks. He slows his step until I am even with them. Eyes me up and down with a crooked smile.

"So you're state, huh?" he says. "Thought so."

"What do you mean?"

"You went to court right? They sent you here?"

"Yup."

"When your parents send you here, you're private. When the court does it you're state. Where you think those clothes and clodhoppers came from?"

"Clodhoppers?"

"Those brogans you got on your feet. Welfare, man! It's all welfare."

"Oh," is all I can say to this.

The word *welfare* reverberating in my head.

I remember getting the day off from school last year. To meet the welfare man when he came. My mother could not be home for him. She had found day work in a few homes in town. To supplement the monthly welfare check. A thing against all the welfare rules. And left me home to tell the welfare man that she was at the doctor's. I spent the morning pretending I owned the house. Sitting there in the jacket from my Sunday suit. Puffing a candy cigar I had gotten from Sherman's up the block. A giddy flight of fantasy. Tempered only by the uneasy fact that it was me my mother had chosen. Confident in the knowledge that I could carry off the lie.

That didn't sit all too easy. I had to get up. Walk the thought of it off. Twice around the room. Then down the hall. Out to the kitchen for some water. Champagne in my rich man's pretense. When I got there, Jackie's door was open. She was in there with a broom and dustpan. Chasing down the last bit of dirt. Making backward circles. Around and around the room. A few rebel crumbs always sliding under the dustpan's battered lip. When she caught me standing there and realized I'd been watching her, she burst out laughing. A genuine and hearty guffaw. A laugh so full of fun, no matter what, I had to laugh too.

She put the dustpan down.

Leaned the broom on the couch.

Gave me the happiest face I'd ever seen.

"Well, that's life," she said. "Sometimes you just can't get all the dirt."

By the time the welfare man showed I had it all worked out. Push come to shove, when Victor was at the door that time, my mother had lied for me. The least I could do was tell this one white lie for her. But welfare remained a whispered word in my house. For all the humbleness of walking with the Lord, neediness was still a thing tinged with quiet shame.

I glimpse around me. Acutely aware, now, of what the other kids have on. All of them in shirts and dark slacks. A few wearing ties. Two decked out in suits. None of them in plaid print polyester shirts. Or turd-brown "clodhopper" shoes. No one else sporting the telltale uniform that marks you as a ward of the state. Not even Pee Wee. And I'm all but certain that he must be state, too.

When we get to the dining hall, the spicy aroma of fried chicken tickles my nose before we even hit the doors. When we do step in I barely recognize it as the same place where I had had lunch. The tables are all draped in white linen. And in the big open space between the door and the steam table there's an extra table set up.

Also draped in linen. On it I see a wheel of bread. A chalice of wine. And what looks like a Bible. The stuff of Communion to me. Like I have seen them do at Straight Gate Church. Only there it's grape juice instead of wine. *So this is what the shower and change of dress is all about,* I tell myself.

A few minutes later a man steps up to the table. He is dressed in black. There is a silvery white shawl draped over his shoulders and a small, brimless cap on his head. Everyone gets to their feet. Stands at attention at the head of their alcoves. The man in black holds the wheel of bread aloft. Breaks it in two. Then the chalice of wine. Holds that aloft, too. Takes a sip. Sets it back down. And starts singing. I can't make out any of the words. It isn't in English. A hymn of some sort, I assume it must be.

I suppose on some level I realize that most of the kids here are Jewish, but not in a way that means anything in particular to me. All I can see is how crisp and sharp everyone looks in their dress clothes compared to me. How much they all look like people of consequence. How bright and shiny their hair looks. How they have all obviously bent over the bathroom sink just before coming and slicked it back with a wet comb.

And as the man in black intones "*Baruch atah adonai eloheinu melech haolam,*" all I can do is gape at those still-damp strands of slicked-back hair—at how they catch the overhead lights and glisten. Framing each fresh-scrubbed face with a shimmering, matinee-idol aura—and rue that I was born on the wrong side of the tracks and into the wrong skin. I see nothing so nuanced and abstract as a subcategory. Only this. These luckier sons.

But the fried chicken, when we get to it, is great.

And there is plenty of it.

"Go on then, Stringer," Pop Bedford says with a wry smile. Watching me suck the last of the meat off the bone. "There's more where that came from."

Pee Wee's eyes go sly when he sees me coming back to the table with another plateful. I see that he and Charley still have half their fish sticks and mashed potatoes left on their plates.

"You shoulda' had the chicken," I tell them. "It's pretty good."

I don't mean anything by it. I don't know that Pee Wee and Charley are Catholic. Much less that Catholics aren't allowed to have meat on Friday. But I see Pee Wee's bottom lip draw up. See his eyes climb from my plate to me.

"Lookit Stringer," he says, eyes dancing in their sockets. "Smackin' his lips on fried chicken. Got his welfare package today. He's never had it so good."

Next thing I know everyone at the table is gaping at me. And my point of view does a complete one-eighty. Not my own eyes I'm looking through anymore, but theirs. Seeing myself sitting there. In my charity-issue clothes. A big, greasy, chicken-eating grin on my face. Like I never had a decent meal before in my life. A Currier & Ives portrait of me. The fried chicken suddenly obscene. My nose rendered bigger and wider than it is. My skin tinted black as coal. My hair a wooly, untamed mess. And me, suddenly more naked, even, than in the shower pit. And smoldering with private shame. Because Pee Wee is entirely right. I've never had it so good.

There is TV after dinner. Everyone in the living room on the first floor. And snacks, too. Every evening, I later learn. I don't hang around for any of this, though. All I want to do is hide myself in bed. I go right to my room when we get back to the cottage. Lie there, staring at the ocean liners on the wall. At the sextant perched atop the radiator cover and the captain's hat crowning it.

12

They are short one choosing up sides for softball. And Andy looks at me moping around near the field and says, "Stringer!" Just like that. Andy's a brusque sort of guy. Thick and barrel-chested. He usually gets to be a captain when it comes to softball because he can pitch. Sort of. I give him a *Who? Me?* look—that's the first dumb thing I do—and he says, "You know how to play, don't cha?"

I say "Yeah," and soon as I say it I wish I had been more forceful about it. Something along the lines of *Of course I know how to play baseball!* But I just say "Yeah."

"Well, get over here," Andy complains.

He turns to do the *once, twice, three, shoot* thing for first ups. Him and the other captain. Steve. A kid who looks like he is straight out of one of the glossy car pictures on the walls inside. They call him "Squeaky" when they want to get under his skin. His voice hasn't finished changing yet. It leaps, when he is excited, to a higher register. They also tease him about his ears. Which are not so big as they make them out to be really. It's just the way he wears his hair. A glorious mop of auburn up top. But cut close to the skull on the sides. So that his ears seem to protrude more than they do. They still call him Dumbo, though, sometimes.

Just about everyone here has that. A not-so-nice second name someone tags you with. These are city kids here mostly. And it seems they aren't happy unless they are in your face about one thing or another. And if you're the new guy, forget it. First I was "Four-eyes." One of the hazards of wearing glasses. So I was used to that. Then I was branded "Sticks." Because I'm from Mamaroneck. "The sticks" as far as everyone here is concerned. And because I use words like "neat" and say "doody" instead of "shit." For a while I was called "Burnt-off." I got that one in the shower pit. I was in there scrubbing up one morning and Pee Wee made a remark about my thing being burnt off. My skin is darker down there when it's all shrunk up from the water.

Little guy or no, Pee Wee gets away with saying stuff like this. Because he's real tight with Charley. The two of them are almost inseparable. And Charley's got that Victor thing going for him. That same dark knack for intimidation. You mess with his friends, he's always saying, you mess with him. So Pee Wee pretty much has free reign to mess with anybody else.

Steve wins the toss and starts counting off the batting order. Andy hitches up his Bermuda shorts. Goes down the line, like a general. Dispatches us to our field positions one by one. He mulls for a second when he gets to me. Drives the nail of his forefinger through the part in his hair. Then says "Right field."

"Right field," I say back.

And when I do I hear a snort over my shoulder.

I turn around and it's Pee Wee.

"Right field, left-out," he says.

I only wonder what he means by that for a second because someone throws me a spare mitt and the game begins. It's fits and starts at first. Mostly because of Andy's pitching. He throws loopers. They come in high above your head then drop down almost vertically at the plate. Every few throws a screaming match erupts. Andy trying to bluster Harvey—the poor sap they roped into being umpire—into seeing it his way. Which is that, since the ball at some point cuts across the batter's shoulders on the way down, it is a strike. Between Andy bullying Harvey and Harvey flip-flopping on his calls and the other team crying foul and the arguing and name-calling that follows, there is little actual baseball action to speak of. And as the inning drags on, I grow more and more antsy for a chance to be in on a play. A chance to show the other kids I've got the stuff. Because for three Saturdays now I have moped by the field while they are choosing up sides. And this is the first time I've ever gotten the nod.

So far my Saturdays have been miserable. The worst day of the week for me. The rest of the week takes care of itself. There is the routine to carry me along, at least. Monday to Friday. Every day the same. Up at six-thirty AM.

Shower. Dress. Make our beds.

Stand by for inspection at 7:00.

Fall out in front of the cottage.

March to the dining hall by 7:30.

Eat breakfast.

March to the AB building for classes at 8:00.

March back to the cottage at 3:00.

March to the dining hall again for dinner at 5:00.

March back home at 6:00.

Snacks at 7:30.

Lights out at 9:00.

And then the whole thing all over again the next day.

Sundays there are visitors. We get to sit with our parents for the afternoon. Have a meal with them. And my mother hasn't missed a visit yet. Even though it is her church day. And even though she has to take two buses and a taxi to get here. It's a squirmy business sometimes. My mother doesn't wear makeup of any kind. Not even lipstick. Or paint her nails. *Christians don't wear makeup*, she says. Makeup is too "worldly." And when she comes to see me here my ears burn sometimes. For how plain and almost masculine her face suddenly seems. Amidst all the other faces. All those glossed lips and rouged cheeks and powdered noses.

Saturdays we get to sleep in an extra hour. And there are chores to do after breakfast. Indoor chores and outside chores. We dust, sweep, mop, wax, shine, prune, water and rake. Until all is spic and span. But after chores are done and there isn't anything anymore that we *have* to do, it's like falling off the edge of a cliff for me. A whole empty afternoon to myself. And no great idea what to do with it. Or who to do it with.

There is a ping-pong table on the porch. But you have to argue and fuss to get your turn. And the last thing I want to do with these guys is argue and fuss. There is the living room. But the TV does not go on until after dinner. Nothing to do in there but lounge. Some of the guys have hobbies. There is a little guy here named Malcolm who's pretty good with a drawing pencil and paintbrush. He doesn't talk to folks much. Just sits and paints. It's always subways. And not just the stuff you see from the platforms either. He knows what's in the tunnels—a world I have never seen and which is brighter and more colorful than I would have imagined. At least the way he sees and paints it.

For most of the other kids it is car models. From fancy kits their parents bring them from the hobby shop. They come with pages of instructions. And hundreds of pieces. And you put the thing together from the inside out. Part by part. Pretty much the same way a real car gets built, I imagine. I have asked my mother to bring me up a kit. But they're expensive. So, I don't know.

Long story short. Saturdays have been mope days until now. And I'm like a firecracker out there. Tensing on every pitch. Leaping at every *thunk* of the bat. Ready to pounce on anything that comes even vaguely near. Thinking *just one great play . . .* One impossible liner snatched out of the air. One good double-play throw. And I won't have to slough through my Saturdays alone anymore.

Five batters in, though, not so much as a dribbler has come my way. And I finally get it. What Pee Wee was referring to. Almost all of us are right-handers. And righties hit to left field. They don't hit to right. Being in right field means being "left out." Of the action. That's why Andy has put me here. The one position where I can do the least damage.

Then Pee Wee comes up to bat. Strides up to the plate. Takes a few fierce cuts with the bat. Does a Babe Ruth. Points the bat at me in right field. Before he settles in the batter's box. And right away, I can feel my pulse start to pound. I drop into a half crouch. Plant my legs apart. Pound my fist into the mitt. Every nerve in my body on alert. If I do nothing else again ever in life I am going to get this ball.

Andy sends his first pitch down. One of his towering sky liners. Pee Wee lays off and on the way down it breaks across his far shoulder. Harvey peers at Andy before he calls it a strike. Pee Wee screws up his face, but doesn't kick up a fuss. Andy throws again. This one's so far off even he can't argue it into being good. Then, on the third pitch, he sends up a lazy looper. And it's near enough. Pee Wee whacks the thing. I see it arch up and bend for the middle ground in front of me. And knowing this is it, all that my life has been and all that it will be converging on this one moment, I bolt after it as if a donkey had kicked me. I can run. There is no dispute about this. My legs are long and my body is light. I can really chew up ground.

Even so I'm thinking, *However fast I may have run before in life, let me be faster than that now!* And, sure enough, that's exactly what I do. I fly infield like a rocket. Faster than I imagine possible. So fast, in fact, that within a matter of a mere second, I completely overshoot the ball. It flies over my head. Lands behind me with a rude *thump!* I spin around. Face and ears on fire. But the center-fielder is already there. He scoops the ball up and tosses it in, holding Pee Wee to a double. Andy screams at me. Something rude and foul. But I don't look at him. And I don't dare even glimpse at Pee Wee.

By the time we get off the field we're three runs down. And there is no rallying back in our half of the inning. Not with Steve up on the mound. He's a left-hander. Fast balls mostly. With a pretty mean curve to back it up. He fires sidewise, his arm whipping down in an arc. His legs snapping together as if he is suddenly standing at attention. The ball taking off from knee high. Snapped with such force that his buttocks quiver and a forward swash of his hair flops down into his eyes. He has to shake it back after every pitch. A nod to glory, in my eyes. A pang goes through me each time I see him do it.

It's a quick inning. Five up and no runs in. Back to the field we go. Only now anyone who can pull the ball makes a purpose of aiming for right, figuring me for the weak spot. And being all the more eager now, wanting so bad to make up for my mistake, I can't seem to do anything right. I manage to snag a ball. A slow roller. But rush the throw to first. It goes wide and bounds into the pines for a ground-rule double that scores a run. I get under a pop-up. Haul it in against my chest. Hold on to it for dear life, thinking, *It may not be pretty but I got it! I got it!* Only, I'm so busy patting myself on the back I miss the guy tagging up on first until it is too late. I gun the ball to second fast enough. But overlooking the guy on third.

He slides home.

And Andy turns snide.

"Thanks a lot, Stringer," he says.

It's all downhill after that. Fatalism sets in. Me out there but not wanting anymore to be out there. Thinking, *Who am I kidding? I'm not going to make any big play. I'm not going to do anything but embarrass myself. All I need is to want something bad enough and it will be for sure denied.* And not just in this game either, I tell myself. It's everything. My whole cursed life. Like the fireman's carnival down at the harbor. Where my mother has taken Wayne and me every summer since we moved to Mamaroneck. And where every year Wayne is quick to snag some prize on the wheel of fortune game. But never me. Even with my mother dropping a good five dollars worth of quarters, sometimes, to win some ten-cent trinket for me. Quarters she can't really afford to waste.

Then a couple of summers ago, Wayne, Michael, Chuck and me, coming from the school playground one evening. And seeing arc lights knifing through the sky. And a crowd of people. When we hit the tip of

Rockland, bottlenecking in front of the temple that had just been built on what had once been "seven hills," a patch of uneven grassy land that we used to play on. Then, nosing our way into the queue, discovering what all the excitement was about. A grand opening, if you will. And the news that Roy Campanella was inside the place.

We all thought that was something. A famous major leaguer visiting our little town. And decided to hang around for a while. Maybe catch a glimpse of him. The next thing we knew we were being handed tickets. And hurried along. Until we found ourselves inside a huge, glistening hall. And ushered to three empty waiting seats.

Roy Campanella was already up on the stage. Flanked by men in dark suits. And when they introduced him, the place went wild. Everyone rose to their feet. And whooped and clapped and cheered as he rolled himself slowly to the center of the stage and waited for them to lower the microphone. A thunderous noise. I didn't take in most of what he said when he spoke. That is, I heard it all—a lot of stuff about beating the odds and never giving up. But I was distracted by the sound of his voice itself. At how frail and humble it was for a hero's voice. That and the wheelchair. I couldn't get over gaping at it. It seemed like the coldest, ugliest thing in the world to me. A cruel reminder that the world is the way it is.

When he was through and the cheering died down, they rolled a huge wire barrel to the center of the stage. It was filled with slips of paper. A man in a black suit and skullcap took position beside the thing. He had a little glass case in his hands. With a baseball inside it. An official major league baseball, he let us know. One that had been signed by Roy Campanella himself. I pulled my ticket stub from my pocket as he instructed us to all do. Saw the long number printed in red at the bottom of it. And tried to cheat fate. By not even daring to hope as the man gave the barrel a few hearty spins. Withdrew a slip of paper. And read off the winning number.

But, no.

It wasn't even close.

Then, no response at all.

Only dry silence.

The man read off the number again.

More slowly this time.

I heard "Over here!"

Wayne. With his eternal luck.

They ushered him up to the stage. Everyone applauding for him. Like he was a big star or something. And he got to shake Roy Campanella's hand. They handed him his prize. No mere trinket this time. Like at the carnival. But a thing I would have given a limb to have won. To march off with it to school that fall. And for once draw the envy of my classmates instead of the other way around. But it had been Wayne. *Wayne!* Of all the people sitting in that auditorium—and there must have been at least three hundred of them—no one could have possibly given less of a fart about baseball than Wayne.

He came back to his seat grinning ear to ear. I said something stupid. Like "Hey!" or "Way to go!" when he sat back down. But I was writhing inside. Jealous. Full of envy. One of those moments between me and him. Me wanting to punch him or hug him, I couldn't decide which. All that. But something else as well. There was God in there too. We were, after all, in a church—a fancier one than I had ever seen before. And filled with a luckier breed of worshipers than the lost and broken lot at Straight Gate—but a church nonetheless. What better place for God to make his point. That, unlike me, Wayne, in choosing to walk with the Lord, had placed himself among the Chosen. That Wayne had been ordained one of his lucky sons too. While I, having run from Him, was to be forever cursed. That nothing I ever reach for will come to be. And seeing Wayne there clutching that ball. A thing for which he had neither hungered nor thirsted. Given only as the gift of his surrender. I thought *punch him. Or maybe slap him congratulations on the back a little harder than necessary.*

He's my brother for crying out loud.

How could he ever choose God over me?

As the next batter gets into the box. Before Andy has thrown the ball. And just as I am deciding that baseball is a stupid game and a waste of time. Marty wanders down to the field and Andy descends on him. Marty's no great athlete either. He's more of a muser than anything else. The kind of guy to ponder stuff the rest of us toss off as not worth the effort. A few days ago, for instance, it had been in the news about the connection between cancer and smoking and Marty—who had heard somewhere that it isn't the tobacco but the paper that gets you sick—wondered aloud, even though he does not smoke, if peeling the paper off a cigarette before you lit it up would solve the problem. I guess he's no great thinker either. All the same, they pull me for him. I don't even get a turn at bat.

Pee Wee snickers something when I walk off the field. Calls me a *doofus*, whatever that means. I stop dead in my tracks and glare at him. Wanting him to say something else. Wanting him to push me over the brink. To push me beyond thinking. If I think, even for a second, I am no good for taking a poke at the next guy. But Pee Wee—*damn Pee Wee!*—doesn't say another word. Just stands there waiting until I slink off the field. Hating him. Hating Andy. Wishing the left-hander's glory could be mine.

13

We're in the van. Charley and me. And Pee Wee's not with us. He's been in the infirmary with the flu for three days. So it's just the two of us this trip. And Charley says to me, "Why don't you come with me, Stringer? To my church?" For two months I had gotten away with spending my Sundays at large. All but a handful of the kids here do their church on Saturday anyway. In the synagogue on campus. For the rest of us there are a couple of vans. To take us each to the church of our choice. But since no one forced me to go, I just let the issue hang. But then my mother caught wind of it. Had them put my name on the driver's list.

I told them whatever is closest, when they asked which church I preferred, and lucked out because the place they dropped me at—this little Episcopalian chapel in town—isn't all that hard to take. I mean the first time was a little shaky. Half the people in there craning their necks around when I walked in the door. And eyeing me over. Though they sent up smiles behind the stares. Remembering where they were. And being it's still church, I still get the feeling, sitting there, of something being required of me. Something for which I don't have any real frame of reference. But it's not at all like the musky, fetid hoedowns at Straight Gate. Where you literally sweat for your sins. It's quieter. More subdued. Very low key.

Boring, even.

So I tell Charley, "Okay. Let's go to your church." Which is the same one Pee Wee goes to. Both of them being Catholics. And soon as I say it, I like the idea.

Charley and Pee Wee and me have been getting along lately. Sort of. Ever since I caught the two of them in the basement storage room a while back. Doing something they shouldn't have been doing. A Saturday. After chores. Pop had told me to put the scratch rakes away after we finished doing the front yard. And when I walked into the storage room, there they were. Puffing away on a Marlboro. We're not allowed to smoke. You can lose your home visit if you do. At the very least get put "on dep." Which stands for *deprivation*. Meaning you lose your privileges. Not that a guy feels all that privileged here in the first place.

Pee Wee started when he saw me. But Charley just looked me in the eye. Helped himself to a slow, deliberate, nonchalant drag. Blew a little cloud my way. Charley can be friendly when he wants to be. But you have to watch yourself when he does. He'll throw little challenges at you every now and then. To see how you handle them. He can smell it out if you are afraid of him, too. And he isn't above leveraging that to his advantage. He isn't too happy when you're not afraid of him, either.

"You smoke, Stringer?" he said.

I lied. Told him, "Yeah, I smoke." And he took another lazy puff. Then another one. I could see he liked having control of the thing. Making Pee Wee stand there and wait his turn. Only he didn't pass it to Pee Wee next. He passed it to me. So I had to take a drag. The two of them looking on with keen interest as I stuck the thing in my mouth and pulled on the filter. I thought of showing off a little. Exhaling through my nose. Like I have seen other guys do. But I decided not to push it. It was hard enough not coughing or gagging on the thing. Obviously my lungs didn't want the smoke in there. It had a nasty, chemical taste too. I couldn't fathom what on earth the appeal was.

Then Charley said. "Go ahead. Take another drag," which I didn't really want to do, but did any way. Not wanting to punk out in front of him. This time I did it. Exhaled through my nose. I was pretty impressed with myself. Except that next thing you know the room started to get elliptical. The floor started to rotate under my feet. And I heard a high whine in my ears. It was all I could do not to vomit.

The thing was, though, it was kind of nice. I mean for as long as the cigarette burned we were just three guys. Having a smoke. Whereas most of the time, here, if there's any conversation at all it's usually snide or sarcastic. With someone like me being the butt of the joke. Especially with Pee Wee. Like I said, everyone here gets on the next guy about one thing or another. Either you are too tall or too short or too fat or too skinny or too dumb or too smart—or too anything, for that matter. And next thing you know someone's flipping it in your face. *Ranking* a guy, they call it. Pee Wee, though, just seems to have a knack for hitting me right where I live when he does it. He even makes a sport of it sometimes. A game called *the dozens.* Which I'd never heard of before. And could just as well do without. Pee Wee's the only one here who ever plays it. And always when we're around a lot of other guys.

"You're so ugly," he'll say, *"that you have to put a sheet over your head at night to let sleep sneak up on you."* Or *"You're so poor, the cockroaches in your house upped and moved next door. You're so black,"* he even said once, *"your mother won't let you cross the street at night."* Everyone howled over that one.

The object of the game is for me to come back at him. Say something even worse about him. But I get all wounded, to tell the truth. When he snaps on me like that. I mean, I *am* poor and ugly and all that. And there *are* cockroaches in my house. Hundreds of them. Living in the hole in the wall under the kitchen sink. And nothing we do seems to get rid of them. And I'm sure Pee Wee knows this, too. Sure he's chased down a few roaches himself. Sure his folks have to scrape to get by sometimes, too. That's the power he has over me. Knowing from his own experience just where to hit me. Only, the way I figure it, none of these other guys need to know about it. I can never bring myself to do like Pee Wee. Tossing around the most private shames between us in public the way he does. Even for a laugh.

Anyway. There was none of this there in the shed. Except, maybe, for Charley trying to catch me in a lie. Grilling me in a casual way about my illustrious smoking career. Asking me out of the blue what brand I smoke when I wasn't expecting it. I was ready for him though. I had seen a commercial for Taretons on TV a couple of times. And the idea that they build a "charcoal chamber" into a cigarette filter kind of grabbed me. So when Charley said, "So whaddaya' smoke," the name just rolled off my tongue.

His face got a little less friendly after that.

"Tareton," he sneered. Like it was the most ridiculous thing in the world. He took the cigarette from my hand. Looked at it. Tossed it on the floor. Ground the thing to bits under his shoe. It wasn't even finished.

"You lipped it," he said.

Later Pee Wee told me that *lipping* a cigarette meant getting the filter end all wet. And that the whole phrase was "you *nigger*-lipped it." But the point is, I was treated better behind a cigarette. Like we were all equals. That's the appeal of the whole thing, I guess.

Anyway I have hung with them a few times since, here and there. Mostly to sneak a smoke together. And when I started going off grounds to church it was the three of us, too. And since we have to wait a while for the van to come after services, I get a chance to pick up a pack of smokes at the store down the block. So now I'm a church-going smoker, you could say. And on my way to Charley's church. Saint something-or-other. To see how the Catholics do it.

It's an intimidating place. All those high, gilded ceilings. And vaulted archways. And tall, painted windows. All that polished brass and purple velvet. And blood red satin everywhere. The priest. All done up in robes. White and gold, shoulder to heel. Silver and rubies on his fingers and neck. I can't imagine him conducting a wedding. You'd have a hard time telling him from the bride.

Charley halts two steps into the place. Dips his fingers in a bowl of water. Sitting on a pedestal just inside the door. Mutters something I can't make out as he taps his forehead and shoulders with them. And just when we're about to sit down, he does it again. Drops to his knees this time. So fast you'd think he'd been shot. Does the tapping and muttering thing again. I almost giggle. It strikes me so funny seeing this. Tough guy Charley on his knees. Only I don't dare because I'm not sure what I should do. Whether I'm supposed to act like a Catholic, being I'm in their church. And be down there with Charley. Or whether that would be a bad thing for a Protestant to do. It's such a tricky thing. This business of trying to make heads or tails of what it is that God wants.

I don't get the service either. All that standing. Then sitting back down. Then standing again. Over and over again we do this. And the sermon isn't even in English. I don't get why the choir is all boys, either. Instead of mostly women. Like at Straight Gate. Just boys. And they all look so bright-eyed and blush-cheeked. Their voices so precious and dainty. You halfways want to go up there and kiss one of them. By the time the whole thing's over, I'm thinking, *Yeah. Episcopalians.*

The van hasn't come yet when we get back outside. It's a pretty delicious thing. Having those few minutes all to yourself. Charley whips out his Marlboros. Shakes a cigarette half out of the pack. Sips it into his mouth. Then, in an absent-minded way, reflex more than anything else, holds the pack out to me. I take one and put it in my mouth. Careful not to engage too much lip.

"C'mon," he says. Before I have the thing half lit. And takes off down the block. I scramble after him. To a little store a few doors away. Every kind of diversion you can think of inside. The shelves crammed with newspapers, magazines, comics, toys, games, hobby kits, novelties. Jars of penny candies lined up on the counter. Licorice sticks. Peppermints. Sour balls. Jawbreakers. Lemon drops. Gum balls. Jelly beans. Rock candy. Mints. A paradise of sweets. And me still holding the dollar my mother gave me to put in the collection plate.

Charley goes straight to the cooler.

"Kind'a soda ya' want," he says.

"Coke," I tell him, thinking *Charley's being generous today.*

He comes back with a Coke in each fist.

The clerk puts down his newspaper.

"Separate or together?" he says.

And this is when I find out Charley's real purpose in inviting me along. He is not impolite about it when he asks if I have any money on me. But he gives me a Victor look. That hooded eye, clenched jaw thing. Obviously impatient for any answer other than *yes,* since I hadn't exactly made a secret of the buck in my pocket. Pulling it out to look at it. Twice. While we were rolling off campus.

"Hold up," Charley says. When I go to fork over the buck. He reaches up to a display to the right of the cash register. And pulls a white, rectangular package from it. "This too," he says. And tosses it on the counter. A package I've never seen before. There is a narrow gold band around the top of it. Just like a pack of cigarettes. An ornately sketched thistle-looking bud below that. *Chewing tobacco?* The clerk punches the cash register. Taps out twenty-five twice. One for each soda. Then a whopping forty-nine cents.

I look at Charley.

"Wow," I say.

He diverts his eyes out the window.

"What is that stuff?"

"Calendar bowzer," it sounds like he says.

The van is idling down the block when we get back outside. We have to ditch our cigarettes. Charley zips the band from the package and peels back the wrapping. I see there are little rectangular slabs inside. Each wrapped in embossed tinfoil.

"Butterscotch," Charley says. "Toffee. It's from England. Want one?"

He drops one of the silvery little pieces of bullion in my hand. The names *Callard & Bowser* embossed diagonally across the foil. And I forget all about being ticked over how he'd coerced me into paying for them. I have never had anything imported before. *Imported* is a word that has always demarked the divide between *them* and *us*. And when I pop the thing in my mouth and its rich flavor bursts on my tongue, I can see why it cost about ten times as much as regular candy. I can actually taste the butter! It leaves me entirely grateful to Charley. For introducing me to such an exotic and classy delight. For letting me in on this secret reserved for luckier sons.

Charley all but sucks his teeth when I ask for another piece. We are back at the cottage. Halfway up the stairs. To change from our church clothes. But he reaches into his pocket anyway. Just as he is handing it to me, his eyes fly over my shoulder.

"Callard & Bowsers?" I hear Pee Wee say.

I turn around to see him at the top of the stairs

His eyes flash from the slab of butterscotch to Charley and then to me.

"You're out," Charley says. "They let you out?"

"For visitors," Pee Wee says, his face going grave. "My moms. She's coming up today."

Nobody says anything for a second. Nobody looks at anyone. It is only Pee Wee's aunt, and sometimes his uncle, who ever come to see him. I have never seen his mom or dad. It is a quirk of this place that none of us talks at all about whatever it is behind our being here. You have to stumble across a moment like this to get any idea.

Charley closes the gap between him and Pee Wee. Hands the package to him so he can have some too. The two of them head off for their room. Pee Wee takes a parting, over-the-shoulder glance at me. There is a look on his face I can't quite read. But I can see it's nothing good.

14

My mother brings along roast chicken when she comes. We eat it picnic style. With our fingers. There is creamed spinach too. And macaroni and cheese. Not anything like the grand feasts I see being relished around me. But my mother makes the smoothest macaroni and cheese. I have not tasted any other that comes even close. We are eating and talking, her, me and Wayne. More eating than talking for me. I find I am having a hard time forming complete sentences.

My mother says, "I take it you're showing me this because you want me to get you one of these."

"Well. Yeah," I say.

She is looking at an advertisement I have just handed her. For an Aurora Deluxe car model kit.

"Didn't you just tell me a few weeks ago that you wanted a transistor radio?" she says.

"Well," I say.

"Yeah," I say.

"And didn't you tell me that if I got you a radio you wouldn't ask me for anything else?"

I see Pee Wee. Sitting in the foyer. Dressed in a clean, white shirt. His eyes go to the front door. Then down.

"Well," I say.

"Yeah," I say.

Pee Wee gazing over at us now.

"So now you're telling me you want this, too." My mother says, deftly separating a piece of chicken from the bone with her fingers. Pinkies arched. And popping it in her mouth. "You want to have your cake and eat it, too."

She puts her eyes directly on me when she says this. Peers over her spectacles and holds me in her sights. She has an entire repertoire of such pithy sayings. Most of them convened around the concepts of *can't* and *doesn't.* There is nowhere you can go with them. It is worse than hearing the word *no. No* implies a decision. Decisions can be reversed. *Can't* and *doesn't* place matters utterly beyond possibility.

I wither under her gaze. Pull my eyes away. Put them instead on Wayne who is glomming down food with alarming gusto. Like he is going to be shot dead in the next instant. He's pretending he's not the least concerned about the conversation. But I know he's getting his jollies out of watching me squirm.

"You'll have to pick one or the other," my mother declares. With finality. "I can't afford to buy you both of them. Money doesn't grow on trees, you know."

She has been using that one for years. The worst of the lot as far as I'm concerned. Why introduce an entirely seductive idea like that on one breath, and on the very next dash it on the rocks? The first time I heard her say it, I was maybe eight years old. I thought *Money tree . . . Wow!* The next day I took a package of seeds I had found in the trash, pounded them one by one into the face of a nickel with a hammer, and planted the thing in the yard. For the next week and a half I tossed in my sleep, nights. Woke up every morning with fresh hope. That this would be the day. I would walk outside. Look down. And there, peeking out of the ground, would be the edge of, say, a fresh twenty-dollar bill. Of course nothing ever sprouted. An empirical lesson for me. *Prima facie* evidence that the fatal spear in the heart of every wish for joy in life is that the world is the way it is.

When I glance towards the foyer again, Pee Wee is not there. His mother never shows. Later, at dinner, I notice he and Charley hissing and frowning at one another. In the throes of some dispute. By the time we are all in pajamas and waiting on lights out, they have cut each other a wide berth. Charley in the TV room. With Pop and some of the guys. Pee Wee with the rest of us. Hanging out around the ping-pong table on the porch.

There is another Steve here. Not the pitcher, but from down the hall. A big-hipped guy who likes to laugh. His last name starts with a "J" so I call him Jay. We have had an on again–off again ping-pong tournament going between us for a while now. I have gotten pretty good at it. I can cut English on the ball. I can get off a good slam. My biggest advantage with him though is serving up one-liners along with the ball. Which I'm doing now. A running commentary really. Like a sportscaster. *How's it looking to you, Burt? Well, Harry, looks to me like the kid pinged when he should have ponged.* Goofy stuff like that. Only I'm five points up on Jay, it's cracking him up so much. Pretty soon we are all pretty much cutting up. Everyone but Pee Wee that is. Then Marty cracks a God joke. Says, "How come God gave colored guys big dicks?"

I flub an easy lob, hearing this. It had never been even suggested to me before that there were any bragging rights associated with being born inside this skin. I immediately think of Victor. That he must have heard this same claim somewhere. And that the thing in the schoolyard was simply him conducting his own blunt, crude research into the matter.

"I don't know. Why did God give colored guys big dicks?" Jay dutifully chimes.

"Because he fucked up on the hair," Marty says. And everyone has a nervous laugh. Eyes dancing back and forth between me and Pee Wee. Who doesn't laugh. But turns to me. The corner of his upper lip going up.

"What are you laughing at," he says. And I know before he utters another word that the whole sentence is going to be *"What are you laughing at BURNT-OFF!?"*

There is another eruption of laughter when he says it. This one directed at me. I can *feel* my face flush.

"Speaking of little things, P-E-E-E W-E-E-E," I say, groping toward a dozens snap I have overheard. Knowing even as it is leaving my lips that I am blundering into the fire. Challenging Pee Wee at his own game. But not caring about this. Wanting to score at least one sting. "You're so short you can play handball on the curb!"

"*Wh-o-o-a,*" everyone sings. And it is better than a laugh.

Pee Wee's eyes narrow.

The smugness drains from his face.

Apparently he doesn't like being the brunt of the joke any more than I do.

But of course it is not over.

"Yeah," he says "Well, you're so poor your mother has to use toilet paper for Kotex."

Bulls-eye again.

Those curious wedges of Kleenex in the trash at home.

So that's what they were.

Another "*Wh-o-o-a!*" from the Greek chorus.

Only this one more drawn out and full of gravity.

Then all eyes back at me. And tense silence.

In all the mocking and ranking and putting each other down we do it is an unwritten code that you don't bring mothers into it. Everything else is fair enough game. Deformity. Stupidity. Even bigotry. But mothers, no. And they are all looking at me because the only respectable response to someone ranking your mother is to pounce on him hard and fast. Make him take it back one way or another. And loud and clear. The only other possibility is to rank his mother back. As down and nasty as you can. Put the dare back on him. Do nothing, though, just stand there and take it, and it is the surest way to get yourself branded a punk.

I do not want to play this game, I say to myself.

Even as my lips start moving.

"At least I have a mother," I hear myself say. "At least my mother shows up."

The rest of what happens comes at me in blurs and flashes.

There is the wounded look I have at last been able to put on Pee Wee's face. It pulls his eyes and lips all out of register. A payback that would be more satisfying if I could only divorce myself from the pain of it. There are the guys watching and waiting—with spook-wide eyes—on what will happen next. There is the thing that Pee Wee hisses back at me. The words all rushing together. One indistinguishable from the next. Except for the last four succinct and utterly clear syllables . . . *french fry fingers*!

Then, everyone howling. Unable to hold back despite the stakes. They have all seen it. Have probably whispered and giggled over it amongst themselves. My mother eating with me on her visit. Picnic style. With her fingers. Her long, white cover-up gloves laying on the table. Her eczema-ravaged hands fully exposed.

Then, everything going white hot. Like a fire behind my eyes. Me wanting to kill Pee Wee. Not hurt him. Wanting to end his life.

Pee Wee seeing this.

Backing away.

Flying up the stairs.

Me after him clumsily. The other someone or something that has taken over my body not yet centered in it.

Down the hallway.

Into my room.

Pee Wee pulling at the bathroom door.

He has cornered himself!

But it is locked. Someone shouts "Hey!" from behind it. Pee Wee lunges for the emergency door. Hits the crash bar and scrambles down the fire stairs. I lose my footing. Careen down the first few steps before I manage to right myself, and he gains a few paces on me. Is already headed toward the back of the house as I reach the bottom stair. I spot the familiar little gray metal box sitting there. The one with the face of a smiling cow imprinted on the side. Reach inside. My fingers wrapping around one of the empty milk bottles in there. Pulling it out. Hurling the thing hard and fast. A line-drive shot. It explodes, with amazing accuracy, just behind Pee Wee's heels.

"The fuck!" he screams. "You crazy!"

He stalks as much as races into the house. I don't follow him. I am suddenly too heavy for my legs. They go out from under me. The thing that has possession of me now fleeing the scene. I sink down, until my butt meets the stairs, and just sit there. Wanting, really, to lie down. To close my eyes and drift. I actually tell myself this sitting there. Hands over my face. That if I could just lay down and go to sleep everything will somehow be all right.

But nothing is all right.

I hear the porch door whine open.

The *thud* of feet against the wooden stairs.

The softer pad of footfalls against the pavement.

"The hell, Stringer," I hear Pop roar, "'ave you flipped your bloomin' cork?" I open my eyes. Pee Wee is standing beside him. A peculiar look on his face. Like he's just this minute been put down on earth for the first time. That and the flesh of Pop's old eyes gathered in a worrying frown. "The devil's wrong with you?"

"Why can't people just leave me alone?" I say. It comes out like a whine. "I've had enough of this. I can't take it anymore. I just want to be left alone."

I put my hands back over my face.

Say this over and over again.

"All right, lad," Pop says, the steam suddenly gone from his voice.

I feel his hand alight on my shoulder.

Then, "C'mon, now, son. It's all right."

In a gentle voice now.

"Come with me. Let's have a walk."

I let him lead me inside and into the living room and sit me down on the couch. He shoos everyone out of the room. Picks up the phone in the foyer. Mutters into the receiver. Then sets it down and sits with me.

"It's just you and me," he says. "Tell me what happened."

But I can't find a way to put it all together so that it will make any sense to him. All I can say is "Pee Wee." That and "I just want to be left alone. Why can't I be left alone?"

After a few minutes a station wagon rolls up. I see it through the window. See two men get out and one of them unload a white jacket. With straps and overlong sleeves. Pop lets them into the living room. They approach me slowly. And with caution. Like the stalwart interlopers I've seen traipsing into dark jungles on *Wild Kingdom.* And they don't speak to me so much as purr as they come near.

Easy . . .

I do not at all resist. As they strap me into the jacket then load me into the back of the car. I am strangely at peace. As they drive me to the AB building. Usher me into one of the offices and motion me to a chair. They undo the straps. But leave the jacket in place. *So long as I behave myself,* they tell me. Mr. Horowitz is brought in to sit with me. He is quiet and calm and focused. Never lets his attention wane as he shows me how to make and inflate a square ball. Completely out of a sheet of paper.

I am totally captivated by this.

"Paper folding," he tells me. "An ancient Japanese art. It's called origami."

I cannot wait to try it myself.

"Show me again," I tell him.

There are phone calls. Twice someone peeks in the door. Sees the two of us sitting there and excuses himself. But mostly it is quiet. I can hear the click of the clock on the wall each time the minute hand advances. Each *click* counting off the moments to whatever will happen next.

On my third try I am able to do it. Take a flat sheet of paper and by simply folding it this way and then that produce a tight little square which, when I hold it in my hand and treat it to a blast of breath, inflates to a square paper ball. You cannot imagine the glory this brings. A moment of almost immeasurable joy and delight.

Half an hour later I hear a car engine chug up and idle. Then the *Chunk!* of its door slamming shut. My pulse quickens. Mr. Horowitz puts up a sigh. And gets to his feet. As two new men halt by the door.

"You need to go with these men, now, Caverly," he says. "They are going to take you where you want to go. Somewhere where you can be alone."

15

. . . Our day *will come,*

If we just w-a-i-t a-while.

Our day will come,

And we'll have ev-ry-thing . . .

We are in the day room, the staging ground for most of our waking hours. A large, open, central space. Walls the color of weak pea soup. A trio of bare, gaping windows along one of them. Looking down on the courtyard below. Each of them fortified with a thick mesh grid. There is a beat-up couch beneath them. Which is where I am parked. Silently singing along with Ruby and the Romantics. Streaming from an unseen radio.

I know all the words.

It's ten o'clock. Time for morning meds. So all of us are here. Scattered about the well-worn tables and chairs. Half of us wearing blue, hospital-issue bathrobes. Street clothes are allowed. But not demanded. And some of us, me included, figure what's the point.

The nurse is out on the floor with her cart. She's a fresh young thing. I like her long lashes and the rush of color in her cheeks. An errant strand of hair bisects her face. Refusing the refuge of her nurse's cap. The blouse of her uniform swells and recedes each time she bends and straightens from her cart. A cart filled with pills and potions in tiny paper cups. A dozen or so of them. Surrounding a pregnant aluminum pitcher of ice water. For a second I imagine myself painting a smiley face with my finger on its sweating side. Like we used to do at Mama's house. In Mama's large, eat-in kitchen. Which was furnished during the magic age of aluminum. Marilyn. Margaret. Adrian. My brother and me. Perched on tubular aluminum frame chairs. Sitting around Mama's big, watermelon-colored, Formica-topped, aluminum table. Our mouths watering. As Mama concocted a batch of Kool-Aid as only she could make it. Two or three flavors blended together in proportions only she knew. Stirred with a long wooden spoon. In a sweating aluminum pot. Paper-thin discs of lemon bobbing on the surface. Ice cubes rattling at the sides. Then served up. In aluminum cups. Tinted metallic blue and red and purple. We painted smiley faces on the sides with our fingers then. Where the moisture had condensed. Me wondering what kind of magic Mama put to work that made her Kool-Aid taste like no other in the world.

The nurse parks the cart next to The Fireman. The fiercest looking guy in the place. He sits, in a bathrobe, off to himself. In a chair by the far wall. My first day here he spent half the evening storming up and down the corridors. Wailing at the top of his lungs. His deep-set eyes so wild and lit up they looked like high beams at midnight in contrast to his walnut skin. There was a kind of Doppler effect as he stalked the corridors to and fro. Made him sound like a siren going off. Having carried the nicknaming habit here with me, I have called him The Fireman ever since. To myself that is. Never out loud.

When he isn't haunting the hall. When they have fed him this liquid stuff so foul and putrid his pores reek of it. He just sits sunk in a chair. Looking desolate as a lighthouse. Staring out at the space in front of him. But cut across his line of vision and his eyes will catch the motion and lock on to you. Holding your every slightest move in such black and bottomless contempt there is no not knowing that you are an inch away from sharp and sudden rage. Wherever he is I try to keep to the opposite side of the room.

The nurse does her routine. Hands The Fireman his dose. The blouse clinging to, then releasing, the curve of her breasts. Then stands sentry. Watches him as he goes through the drill to show her he isn't faking it. Swallows. Pokes out his tongue. Wags it from side to side.

The medication they give you puts a fog on your brain. Makes it hard to think clearly. When the doctor calls you into his office all he wants to know is how you're feeling. But with that stuff in you it's like your feelings are out there somewhere. You reach for them but they are always just beyond your grasp. Which isn't to say that I don't always gulp my pills right down. I would take more of them if they asked. I am in a hospital after all. The place where they make you well. Why get in the way of that?

The nurse doesn't notice the little tic go off at the edge of The Fireman's eyes. As she crosses in front of him. Doesn't see those dark little orbs slave themselves to the dance of her movements. As she moves on to the next guy. A chubby, pale-faced mope who always wears a yarmulke. Always sits in the same hard-backed chair all day. Legs gathered under him. Elbows tucked into his thighs. Constantly rocking forward and back. Chanting, with relentless regularity, *"S-E-T Schmuck!... S-E-T Schmuck!... S-E-T Schmuck!"*

He halts his mantra as the nurse nears. A Christmas morning brightness dawns on his tortured face. A look surely left over from some other, earlier life. I know exactly what he is going to say. He says it each time the nurse comes around with her cart. The second of only two things, other than his mad, lonely chant, I have ever heard him utter. He also says it at every meal. Perched as always at the head of the table. A nurse right by his side. To coax him into eating, which he never seems inclined to do. A thing that makes me wonder why he is so plump.

"My mother is coming today," he sings.

It spooked me hearing this for the first time. Just hours after getting here. Barely half a day after the thing with Pee Wee. I had to stop and ask myself, *Did he say that?* I thought I had gone mad myself. *Pee Wee's words? Coming out of this guy's mouth?* Of course just like with Pee Wee his mother never comes to see him. Mine either. You are not allowed visitors during observation.

The only other thing that ever comes from his lips, he says during meals. *"I did good today,"* he'll brag. Whenever he manages to actually chew down a few forks full. Mouth open all the while. After which, nine times out of ten, he then vomits back up. I've gotten used to this by now. It no longer disturbs my meal. Except perhaps those runny eggs they serve at breakfast, which never go down so easy in the first place.

He pops the pills and gives the nurse a happy, docile smile. No need for the nurse to bird-dog this guy. No tongue wagging necessary. She could hand him a dose of cyanide and he would cheerfully swallow it down. A sip and a swallow of water and he is back at it again.

"S-E-T Schmuck! . . . S-E-T Schmuck! . . ."

Now it is *Hey Paula o*ver the public address system.

Hey Paula

I want to marry you . . .

Hey, hey Paula,

No-one else will e-ver do . . .

Only breezy, soothing music here. Never anything else. It flutters down from the rafters all day. Every day. You can't get away from it. After a week of this, jacked up on meds all the while, I'm at the point where I'm eager and happy to succumb to its kitschy thrall.

I've wai-ted so long

For school to be through . . .

Paula, I can't wait no more for you . . .

Singing along. Under my breath. My eyelids drawing themselves down like a shade. That all-is-right-with-the-world sensation oozing over me. Snuggling deeper into the couch. Sinking into its soft, pillowy contentment. I can picture them sharp and clear. Paul and Paula. See his glimmering, jet black hair. Swept back in a perfect ducktail. See her adoring eyes. Lashy and mesmerized as he sings to her. Both of them perfectly young and perfectly handsome. And perfectly in love. I embrace the pangs of envy and longing this sends through my gut.

The sweet pain of it as close as I can dare hope come to ever feeling their perfect happiness.

Then I hear it.

—A crash.

—A sharp shriek.

—A sudden splatter of motion.

My eyes pop open. I see a snowy blur. A pair of beefy orderlies racing past me. I see only their backs as they scramble down the long narrow corridor. Their key rings sounding off like alarms. My eyes jump to the chair against the wall. The chair in which a second ago The Fireman was slumped. It is empty, now, lying on its side.

". . . S-E-T Schmuck!. . . S-E-T Schmuck!. . ." the yarmulke guy drones. Louder and faster now. His head dipping down and up like an oil rig. *"Whoop!"* goes the guy sitting next to him. A withered, white-whiskered coot. Who never manages to keep his bathrobe completely closed. *"Whoop!"* he goes again, slapping the arm of his chair. Starts howling like a mad wolf. Then calamity down the hall. The *splat* and *thud* of bodies and limbs against the hard linoleum floor. A long, piercing, mournful banshee wail. Summoned from depths only a lifetime of confounded agony could have wrought. Screaming down the corridor. Jerking half a dozen of us to our feet. *This must be it,* I think to myself. *God's revenge on me. I must be in hell.*

16

They took me straight in to see the doctor when they first brought me here. A long, unnerving walk through the lobby to the elevator, me bundled down like Jack the Ripper. A squeaky ascent to the upper floors. The elevator doors *sloshing* open on a small reception area. Bathed in overhead fluorescents. Which always make me think of night. Never day.

I was unstrapped and sat down.

"The doctor will be right with you."

I stared at the bare, beigey walls. Their vast, flat blandness interrupted by a single, framed, melancholy, autumnal print. A stand of tall, white-barked birches. Stretching up from a brown and orange sea of fallen leaves.

"A long, unnerving walk through the lobby and then this . . . sadness."

Then the doctor appearing. Stretching out his hand. Offering me a smile. Not too much of a smile. Not too friendly. But as it should be. A comforting kind of smile. He's going gray at the temples too. Just as a doctor should.

His crisp white jacket . . .

The nameplate affixed to its pocket . . .

His big, tidy desk . . .

The large tortoise-rimmed spectacles lying in wait upon it . . .

The shelves full of books all the same color . . .

Everything exactly as it should be.

A long, unnerving walk through the lobby.

Then sadness.

Then . . . gratefulness.

Sat me down. Read through some papers. My file, I supposed.

"You are quite the angry young man," he said, looking up. As if expecting a reply. But since it was a statement, not a question, I said nothing. Only sat there waiting.

"Tell me about it," he said, another half-smile creasing his cheeks.

"Tell you about it," I said back. My mind still on intake, not output.

"Yes," the doctor said. "Yes. What are you angry about?"

A question no one had ever thought to ask me before.

One I'd never even thought to ask of myself.

What *am* I angry about?

All sorts of stuff. Sometimes everyone and everything. Mostly it is that it is never not there. Always lurking just beneath the surface. Just waiting on someone or something to attach itself to. Even when I'm feeling okay and things are not so bad, it is there.

All this trudged through my brain without actually reaching my lips.

"Can you tell me *who* are you angry *at?*" the doctor tried.

I went down the list.

My mother, of course, sometimes.

What kid doesn't get ticked at his mother every now and then?

My father. Sometimes, too. Even though he's not around.

My brother . . .

My schoolmates . . .

My teachers . . .

Sometimes everyone and every thing.

"There's this one kid in my cottage," I decided he needed to know, "who just seems to make it his business to mess with me. Just seems to go out of his way to get under my skin."

"Good," the doctor said. Me wondering what was good about it. "Tell me about this Pee Wee."

I did as he asked. I told him all about it. Maybe not the dozens thing. About the cockroaches and wads of Kleenex and stuff. But enough that it felt good. Getting it off my chest like that. To have someone listen, at least. There is Mrs. Mendelsohn. She listens. My caseworker. Everyone at sleepaway school has one. I see her once a week. I like her, too. She seems to really care about me. Always wanting to know how I'm doing. How I feel about how I'm doing. When I sit down with her, though, it always gets into me, maybe because I like her, to put her mind at ease. I'm always telling her I'm doing fine.

I told him about the crack Pee Wee had made. About my mother's hands. How it got me so mad that for a second I really felt like killing him. And his eyebrows gathered. I could see the wheels turning in his head. The pen moving on the pad in front of him. I quickly added, only finding the words in that instant, that I didn't remember being angry so much when I seized the milk bottle. That what I remembered feeling most at that point was an awful weight on me. As if the world was suddenly too heavy for my back. And that all I really wanted, throwing the bottle at Pee Wee, was to drive him and his whole bother off. So I could just sit down there on the stairs.

"I was just so tired," I told him. Of everything. Beyond even being angry. "I felt so. . . weary."

Weary. The word just slid out of my mouth. Not a common word in my vocabulary. But one tossed around pretty good at Straight Gate. It's ever the scourge of the unrepentant, to hear them tell it. One of the inevitable wages of sin. "*Come unto Me,*" they warble, speaking for the Lord in the songs they sing, "*and I will give you rest.*"

The doctor sighed and put down his pen. There was a long, silent minute of him just looking at me. Then a smile. A half-baked one this time.

"Well," he said. "You are here for observation. We shall see what we shall see."

They checked me in. Put me in hospital blues. Left me to wander the patient side of the ward. At the top of the corridor I noticed a man standing in the corner. Hunched against the wall. An older guy. With a balding pate that suited him somehow. He waved *come here* to me and I moved a little nearer. Saw he had a quarter pinched between his fingers. Tapping on the door of the fire alarm box with the thing. He *shushed* me with a finger to his lips. Peered over my shoulder for prying eyes. Waved me even closer.

"I'm sending a message to John Glenn," he confided. In a hoarse, solicitous whisper. Every Abbott and Costello nut-house routine I ever saw flashed through my mind when he said it. I had to struggle to keep a straight face. He tapped away. A grim and determined look on his face. Turned to me at one point to ask if there was anything I wanted to add. I shook my head *no.* He gave it a few final thoughtful taps.

"There," he said with a flourish. "Now, what was your name?"

"Caverly," I told him.

He told me his name too. Which I have since forgotten. Always thinking of him as The Astronaut.

"I could do with a smoke, Caverly," he said. "How about you?"

It was a disarming flash of charm. Him using my first name so readily. As if we were already old friends. And a cigarette sure sounded good. The only problem was that smoking here is strictly a do-it-yourself business. There aren't any store-bought cigarettes. Only the loose tobacco and rice paper they give you to roll your own. A thing that I have yet to pick up the knack for. Went into the day room. Where The Astronaut had himself a good laugh. Watching me litter the table with paper wads and tobacco crumbs. I jumped when he grabbed my hand in mid-roll. Wondering *what's this about?*

"Hold on a minute," he said.

He rose and left the table. And returned clutching a copy of *Life* magazine, a pencil and a piece of Scotch tape. I have no idea where he got them. He sat down. Tore a page from the magazine. Folded it in half, longwise. Taped the pencil to one end of it. Then showed me how to roll a nearly perfect cigarette with the thing in two steps. It worked like a charm. You never know when you'll learn something new.

I carefully removed another page from the magazine.

"You think that's something, check this out," I told him. And proceeded to show him how to make a square ball out of paper and blow it up. The damnedest thing he ever saw, he told me.

We have been as close as you can come to being pals here ever since. He doesn't really strike me as being crazy at all. Except for when he's off communing with the ether in Morse code. *Maybe it's because he's been here awhile,* I tell myself. *Maybe he's getting better.*

17

All of us, except for the guy in the yarmulke, are on our feet now, rubbernecking down the corridor. The two orderlies have The Fireman collared. Are dragging him, kicking and screaming, down the hall. They hoist him against the wall. Shoulder him into his little room. Then slam the door behind him. A jingle bell jangle follows as they fumble through their key rings.

There are not enough beds to go around here. I was lucky enough to get the last free one. Some of the patients have to sleep on mattresses on the dormitory floor. You have to be careful getting out of bed in the morning not to step on one of them. There are single rooms, too, along the corridor. All of which lock from the outside. And each has a wired glass window cut into the door. So that they can see inside. Pretty much a reverse pecking order here. With private rooms reserved for guys like The Fireman. For those who are too far gone.

Ten minutes later all evidence of the uproar is gone. The chair is righted. The mess down the hall is cleaned up. The cart is put back in its bay to wait upon its midday rounds. The head nurse, who had been standing one leg in, one leg out of her cubicle. Eyebrows practically up to her scalp through the whole thing. Returns to her perch behind the glass. And the overhead speakers spray another ditty into the room.

I hear the Drifters sing,

When this old world
starts getting you down
and people are just too much
for you to faaace . . .

As everyone settles back into their trances.

". . . S-E-T Schmuck! . . . S-E-T Schmuck! . . ."

I have to fight inertia. Drag myself off the couch. No one paying me any particular mind. As I dawdle down the corridor. Stop in front of The Fireman's door. And sneak a peek through the wired glass. I see him standing on his bed. Completely naked now. His dark skin vivid against the blinding whiteness of the walls. His huge nostrils are flared wide. His chest is heaving. His arm is pumping feverishly. And there is what looks like a pained expression on his face. As he jerks frantically on his penis. I pull my eyes immediately away. Escape back down the hall. Retreat to the familiarity of my spot on the couch. The image of him grunting away cutting into my brain. As sharply as that *Negro Slave* etching back in third grade.

A long, unnerving walk through the lobby.

Then sadness.

Then gratefulness.

And now this.

A reflection of my own . . . ugliness.

On my tenth day they come for me. I am to see the doctor again, they let me know. He is wearing a too-bright red tie when he shows. It is slightly askew.

"How are you feeling?" he says. "I expect that you have been able to get some rest here, at least."

I mull the significance of *at least* as he plants himself behind his desk and scans the report in front of him.

"Tell me," he says, not looking up, "do you still feel that you are . . . weary?"

It's a peculiar sensation hearing this word fed back to me. It does not at all fit on the doctor's lips. At our first session. When I told him about Pee Wee. About feeling mad enough to want to kill him. A light had gone on in his eyes. *Homicidal rage.* Something he can sink his psychiatric teeth into. But *weariness . . .*

"I have good news for you," he tells me and I am reminded, when he says it, of my mother's words when she came to collect Wayne and me from Mama's house. "We are releasing you," he says. "You are going home!"

"Home," I say thinking, *Mama's house. Palmer Avenue. Hawthorne Cedar Knolls.*

"Yes, we haven't found any real problems," he says. "Nothing we need to handle here at any rate." He smiles yet again. A smile I do not mistake for anything but the pleasantry it is. "It'll just take a bit to make out the papers and we'll have you on your way."

I am taken to gather my things. Not that there are any things, really, to gather. Then seated in the beigey paleness of the outer room. Amidst the hushed bustle of people going about mournful tasks. The sky looks ugly and mean-spirited through the window across the room. And looking at it I discover I am not inclined, after a week and a half indoors, to brave the whims of nature. That I cannot find the necessary effort.

"Mr. Stringer," someone says.

A nurse. One of the outer-office minions.

"They're here."

Down in the lobby I can see the car waiting just outside glass doors. The same boxy wagon I came in. But a different driver behind the wheel. A steady, gray-green drizzle begins to fall as we roll away from the hospital. When we get to the parkway we have to slow to a funeral crawl. It is nose to bumper for what looks like a mile ahead. The driver sighs and mutters under his breath as we inch along. But I'm in no particular hurry.

Gradually the cause of the gridlock labors into view. A circus of flashing red lights. Transformed, by the rain-spattered windshield, into bright rivulets of blood. A pair of idling ambulances. Rear doors open wide like wings. Waiting to swallow up the dead. Two mangled road machines. Locked in an inexorable embrace. A small army of men in yellow rain slickers. Crawling over the scene.

As we coast abreast of this grim tableau I can hear, above the windshield wiper's *weekaw weekaw* tattoo, a hollow moaning. I peer through the window. See him lying there on the sodden pavement. See him writhing in pain as the emergency crew hovers over him.

And then we break free.

The driver leans back into the seat. His shoulders slacken. We sail forward at a healthy clip. Not long after that we are through the front gate. And rolling up the sloping drive. The rain has relented. But the AB building looks cold and ominous as it looms into view against the still-mean sky. We pull in. I get out. We go inside. Down the hall. To the door marked Officer of the Day.

The OD, Mr. Dumphy, puts out a hand.

Welcomes me back with a rogue's smile.

"Pretty scary place, huh?" he says. Dumphy being Dumphy, retired detective that he is, this is less about sympathy than a cautionary note. "Bet you won't wanna go back there."

I give him the answer he's looking for. Nod a vague "Yes." There's no way to explain to him. That being locked down on a ward full of madmen wasn't really the scary thing. Coming to realize that the Grasslands Hospital psychiatric department had no miracle in store for me—that I was to be shipped back to sleepaway school at the end of my stay unchanged—was harder to take. The scariest thing of all, though, was discovering the sublime satisfaction I got out of life in a bathrobe. How willingly my desire for anything more than that had surrendered to the allure of blissful nothingness.

We walk back outside. To Dumphy's car. It's plain and black. Like a hearse. He shuts the door behind me when I climb inside. And it at last registers. A feeling like having been cast out of Eden. That I'm back. Back at sleepaway school. Back in the real, untamed world. Where sometimes things collide violently. Where sometimes agony lies in wait on the road. And where sometimes the sound of your own low moaning is the only sign that you're still kicking.

The proportions are all off a hair when I get back to the cottage. Despite that I have only been away a matter of days. Some things are smaller, some things larger, than in memory. I stare down the looks I get. The appraising glances. Which seek to know if maybe lunacy shows. Greet them with a strange, inexplicable immunity.

At lights out the bed feels strange when I get into it. I cannot fall asleep. I lay on my back. Watching and listening to the silence. Trying to place myself firmly in space and time. Only to discover—with a rising sense of alarm—that I can only manage to do this fleetingly. Enough moonlight bleeds in through the square pane in the emergency door across from me. I can make out the dimensions of the room. I can see my hand when I put it in front of my face. *A large hand,* I notice. With long, big-knuckled fingers. *An often clumsy hand.*

There is this evidence. Plus the sound of my breathing. To assure me that I am, at this moment, here. In my bed. On the second floor of Cottage Five. But it holds no lasting weight. If I cease taking conscious inventory I dissolve back into nothingness. I become again invisible. If the doctor were here right now I would tell him *happiness* is what I'm always so mad about. That it always seems to be someplace else.

18

Every Tuesday after school I sit and fidget in the chair next to Mrs. Mendelsohn's desk while she asks me things. Mostly how I am doing. How I *feel* about how I'm doing. She has been particularly solicitous of my well-being since I've been back.

"And how are things going with you?" she says. "How are you coming along?

I kind of shrug it off. Tell her I'm okay. And she just sits there for a moment like she does. Waiting for more. I know I'm supposed to tell her stuff. She being my caseworker and all. But it's a hard thing for me to do. There are all sorts of things I think when I'm with her. But don't say. You could probably fill a book with them.

"Getting along with everyone?" she says. "The other kids? Your teacher? Mr. and Mrs. Bedford?"

I tell her, "Yeah, I'm getting along okay." Which is pretty much true. The other kids in the cottage have been cutting me a little more slack since I've been back. Even Pee Wee has been off my case. I guess a little frothing at the mouth can be as handy as a quick pair of fists.

And a swell of fondness came over me to see Pop Bedford again. He seems to have himself a good time of it. Being father to us all. The other day we were walking to the dining hall. All decked out and spit and polish for the Friday thing. And I heard him say, "You'd make a good soldier there, lad."

I turned around. Not sure it was me he was talking to. There was a sly kind of twinkle in his baggy eyes. And he let them drop down to take in my shoes.

"A good soldier never looks behind," he said.

It took me a second or two before I realized what he was getting at. That I had missed the back of my shoes with the polish. And when I looked back at him to let him know I got it, he nodded. A stern nod. But with the spark still in his eyes. And I grinned at him. Even though he was sort of scolding me. A cozy, cared-for and cared-about kind of grin I'd say it was.

I don't tell Mrs. Mendelsohn all this. I just tell her I like Mom and Pop pretty okay. That I like the way Pop calls you *lad* and *son* sometimes when he talks to you. And even this little bit gets me in trouble. Because the next thing I know Mrs. Mendelsohn has leaned forward. And she's asking me about my father. Talk about throwing a bucket of cold water on things.

"Tell me something about him," she says.

What's there to tell? I've only laid eyes on the guy twice in my whole life. I don't really know much of anything about him. Except what I have gotten from the things my mother will say. Which, if you put them together, pretty much tell me that I'd do well not to follow in his footsteps.

But Mrs. Mendelsohn keeps at it. Asking questions. And one thing after another I end up telling her about that Christmas. I think I was about nine at the time and Wayne was ten. That one great happy Christmas. When my mother had gotten us off relief. A thing that as a matter of pride she had been determined to do. And had found a clerical job that paid pretty good. At Grasslands Hospital, of all places. Not the psychiatric department, though. Another building altogether. Where they do non-medical stuff.

Anyway, she was working. Which was great as far as Christmas was concerned. Since it meant she had more money to spend. And when Wayne and I woke up Christmas morning there were tons of brightly wrapped gifts under the tree. More than either of us ever could have imagined. Not just the practical stuff we got every year either. Like long johns and socks and gloves. But a splurge of kid-friendly loot. I got a tiny remote control car. With headlights that actually worked. An HO scale-model train set. Complete with a tiny depot and coal quarry. A racing set. A fire truck. Games. Puzzles. Stocking stuffers. Sweets.

I don't remember all the things Wayne got. Only that he never let me play with them. But topping everything off were the two corrugated cardboard, coffin-shaped boxes leaning against the wall. Too big to wrap, my mother told us to open them last. But from the shape of the boxes alone I knew what they were. I had seen the thing on TV.

The year before around Christmas time the Remco Toy Company had put out a *Rifleman* "action set." It came with a carbine "repeater" rifle. Just like Chuck Conners used on the show. A six-shooter. A holster with silver bullets. A pair of spurs. A sheriff's badge. And a replica of a white Stetson hat. When I saw the commercial I dreamed of having one of them. Tooling around the neighborhood. All done up as The Rifleman. Proving to all the other kids that for once we had not been visited by a lesser Santa than they. I went to sleep with my fingers crossed that Christmas Eve. But it wasn't in the cards.

Since then they have put out an army action set, too. And thrilled as I was when Wayne and I opened the boxes and found a Rifleman set for each of us inside, I half wished my mother had split the difference. So that we'd have one army and one cowboy set between the two of us. Though it would be an outside bet whether Wayne, being Wayne, would ever agree to trade with me for a day or so.

We spent the whole afternoon in the spirit of the Wild West, Wayne and me. We must have killed each other two dozen times. Then, late in the evening, as we were winding down. Sated and sleepy. The doorbell sounded. My mother's brow wrinkled. Wondering *Who can that be?* And she pulled herself off the couch with a sigh. I trailed her into the hallway. Hope rising in my chest. Twice before, he had suddenly appeared on Christmas Eve. This man my mother knew. And whom Wayne and I only knew as Bill. I guess he liked my mother. Because he was awfully kissy-poo with her both times. But he also liked to drink. Always had a flask with him. Right in his hip pocket. And drinking being a sin, my mother of course wouldn't let him get to first base with her.

Last time he showed, after Wayne and I had been put to bed, things got a little ugly. My mother had to call the cops to get him out of the house. I listened intently to the mounting rumpus. Staring at the closed door. As my mother made it ever more loud and clear that he was to keep his distance.

I thought Bill was okay enough. Tall. Slim. Good looking. And always in an expensive-looking suit. But that was only part of the reason why I half wished, as I strained to catch the odd word from them through the bedroom door, that my mother would find it within herself to relent. It was the idea of it, more than anything. The idea of Bill maybe standing in as a father. At least for one day. To make the picture of Christmas complete.

"Who is it?" my mother called through the door.

"It's me," I heard Bill's voice say. Wanted to hear him say. Wanted it to be him out there. More than anything. Because even though I was only nine, I had already figured out that maybe the reason my mother never smiles that much is because down deep she's really lonely.

So that's what I heard.

Bill through the door saying, "It's me."

A swirl of snowflakes rushed in when my mother opened the door. I heard her say "Oh My God . . ." as I ducked behind her hip. When I peered back around again I was as shocked as she was. *My father.* Standing there. In a long wool overcoat. Collar turned up. A thick gray scarf wrapped around his neck. His arms flared out. A coffin-shaped, corrugated cardboard box under each one. I have no idea by what miracle it had got in him to come. Nor by what magic it had occurred to him that the thing to bring for Wayne and me was a Remco army action set for each of us.

"What a wonderful story!" Mrs. Mendelsohn smiles when I finish. "Thank you for sharing it with me," she says. And I'm happy that I've put a smile on her face. Happy, too, to see by the clock on the wall that my hour is up.

"See you next week, then?"

"Yep," she says. "Same time. See you." But then her brow bunches. "Oh. One other thing. I almost forgot. We have a new boy coming next week. He'll be in your cottage. And we're trying to decide where to put him. I meant to ask you earlier. How do you get along with Marty and Bruce?"

I tell her they're okay.

"Are the three of you very close?"

"I wouldn't say close," I tell her. "But we get along."

"Because we might have to do a little switching around. You may get moved to another room. How would you feel about that?"

She puts up her serious face when she asks this. Like it's something I should be all concerned about. But I don't see any big deal about it. When you come right down to it, Marty and Bruce are a pretty dorky pair. And being in with them, it is left for everyone to assume we are all of a kind. So it's really no sweat off me, moving.

I don't tell her all this.

I just say I'd feel okay about it. No problem.

And she says, "Fine."

I also never tell her the rest of the Christmas story. How I was sure, considering how magical it all seemed, that my mom and dad would get back together. That we would at last live like a regular family and all would at last be well. I never tell her how I even looked at the picture of Him on the mantel and asked that He would do this for me. But of course, me not being in good standing with Him, it never happened.

Nor do I tell her about how I started picking on Wayne that evening. While we were all sitting there. Even though he hadn't done anything to me. Or that even after my mother scolded me to stop I just kept at it. I don't know why. Until my father rose from the chair he was sitting in. Grabbed me by the arm. And gave me a couple of hard smacks on the butt. I don't tell her all that. I did tell her, though, that there never was a Christmas quite as perfect as that.

19

This new kid. This Walter. Right off the bat Pee Wee started in with him. Jumping on his wimpy name. Calling him *W-a-a-l-l-l-ter.* Like a mother calling you in for dinner. *Green Walter.* Even greener than I was when I first got here. *Walter with the funny shape.* Hips and butt way too big for the rest of him. From day one it was a cinch he'd be in for a lot of flack.

But this . . .

I'm lying in bed half asleep when I hear a noise. Just outside the door. But when I look, I see nobody there. Only the quiet, empty hall. I'm in the middle room now. They gave Walter my old bed and moved me here. Right opposite the top of the stairs. So I can see right into the hallway. It's the smallest room in the house. All the others have three or four beds. This one has only space enough for two. One on either side of the doorway. It's stood empty since I've been here. And I thought I was going to have it all to myself when I first moved in. But halfway through making up the bed I heard someone say "Hey" and turned around. It was the left-hander. Standing in the doorway.

"Steve," I said. A huge, pregnant, canvas duffle leaned against his calf. His pitcher's mitt peeking out of the mouth of the thing. He eyeballed the room. Like a guy checking into a hotel. "So," he said. On the wind of an escaping sigh. "You're gonna be in here too, huh." It was a statement more than a question.

I nodded *yes* anyway. A curt, apprehensive dip of the head. That left me to regret right afterward that I had neglected to put up a smile as well. I made up my bed. Using the shortcut I had learned. Putting hospital corners on the sheets and blankets all at once instead of one at a time.

Marty had shown me this. Bruce, of course, didn't approve. *"It ain't regulation,"* he complained. Marty just sucked his teeth. *"Regulation Schmegulation,"* he said.

When I finished fumbling with my bed I sat on it and watched as Steve slowly laid out his things. Vivid blue denims. Pastel-tinted tees. Brightly colored cotton shirts. Supple, beigey khakis. Snow-white sneakers. The way he handled them, carefully folding each item and smoothing out the wrinkles before placing them in his locker just so, they seemed precious somehow. Each a thing of substance. In and of itself. Even his BVDs seemed more downy and fleecy than any I had laid eyes on before.

Then I felt a little silly. Like a voyeur almost. Sitting there. Just watching him. And tried for a little small talk. Only I couldn't seem to find my way to anything interesting to say. Just my own anxiousness. Ringing back in my ears. And he one-worded me back. Offered me only *yups* and *uh-huhs.* Nothing to invite further conversation. I finally gave up trying. And went downstairs.

It bothered me though. I mean if you're going to share a room with someone you can be friendly at least. It bugged me all day. All during snacks. And while we were all in the living room watching TV. I kept looking over at him. Expecting, for some reason, that he would at least glance back. A silly thing. But I couldn't stop doing it. And of course he never did look back.

When we were both in bed and it was lights out I gave him a "Good night," and he said "Night" back. Which is pretty much all there was to say back. But I felt shortchanged when he rolled over. Putting his back to me. Then I couldn't get to sleep. I was all edgy. Even long after he was dead to the world. One minute I had that kind of quivery feeling you get when you know something's coming your way. A little like you have the night before Christmas. And the next minute the bottom seemed to drop out of everything.

The next morning I was a little slow on the move. After staring at the ceiling all night. But he was up and off to the showers in a flash. As if he couldn't wait to get out of the room. When I finally did gather myself and go down he was on his way up. And when I got downstairs, the shower room mirrors were cruel with my reflection. They showed me only the ruder angles of my face. And the rash of acne that has started to sprout on my cheeks. I soaped up and showered. Then soaped up again. Hell bent on washing away I don't know what. When I got back up to the room, he was gone.

There it is again.

Someone definitely outside the doorway now.

On the landing.

I lower my lids just enough. Keep a watch through the lashes. And see someone. Charley. Hustling up the stairs on tiptoes. *Back from sneaking a smoke,* I suppose. And wonder why Pee Wee isn't with him. They're like *Frick and Frack,* as my mother would say. They do just about everything together. Like partners. A thing I kind of like about them. And which I suppose is part of why it nearly grieves me that for the three weeks I've been in this room, my new roommate and I have mostly seen each other in passing. Except for Saturdays, during chores, when we both have to spend an hour or so cleaning the room.

Half the time he turns in early. While the rest of us are watching TV. When I come up he's already dead to the world. And in the mornings it's like a race to put himself together and be gone. It's like an awkward pantomime. Each of us fumbling to navigate around the fact of the other's presence. I don't think we've said more than five words at a time to each other yet.

Now I hear the hiss of whispered words down the hall. A rustle of sheets. Then bedsprings squeaking. And a few seconds later, the muffled squeak of bare feet on the floor. I peer through my lashes again. And see a small exodus. Maybe half a dozen kids slinking toward the stairs. No one stops to invite me along as they file past my doorway. But whatever is going on I don't want to be left out. I scramble out of bed anyway. And follow the last of the pack. We go down to the main floor. Edge cautiously past Mom and Pop's closed door. Descend to the basement and into the shower room. It feels dank and haunted in the darkness. The scent of disinfectant bites at my nostrils. At the first stall everyone suddenly halts. There, half bent over the toilet, pj bottoms around his ankles, Pee Wee behind him pumping away, is the *new* new kid. Walter. He screws his head around and sees us standing there. Watching Pee Wee hump him. And Pee Wee makes a show of it. Treats us to a sly grin. Turns slightly. So we can see that his thing is really up there.

"What does this mean?" Walter cries to the ceiling. Face scrunched-in with angst. Head bobbing to Pee Wee's rhythm. "What does this mean?"

No one answers. No one seems to know how to react. There is a snicker. From Richie. Red-haired Richie. A half snort that's an orphan as soon as it's born. His freckles gathering back together as he abandons his half-formed smirk. The rest of us just stand there. Gape-mouthed. Our eyes go from Pee Wee to Walter. Then collide with each other. Aware that some fleshy, squishy, act is taking place. Then hit the floor.

A second or two of silence and Pee Wee backs off. Tucks himself back in. Steps out of the stall. And saunters out of the shower room. Walter plops down on the commode and shuts the door. One by one we peel our eyes away. File out of the shower room. Snake back up the stairs.

I get back into bed. Wide awake now. Lay there. Charting the flight of whispers down the hall. Wondering, as Walter had, *what does it mean?* But the implications of what I have just seen, and Pee Wee's brazenness about the whole thing, are too much to tackle.

I feel suddenly lonely.

You would think Marty and Bruce had gotten me used to being odd man out. Third wheel that I was with them. But it is different with just two people and such a close room. The silence is so much louder. More personal, somehow.

Then I feel suddenly angry.

I glare across the room. At the face protruding from the top of the blankets there. A blur of creamy paleness, topped by angry hair. Oblivious and indifferent. As if there isn't a care to be had in the world. And think *well screw you too.* It's so familiar, my abrupt splash of enmity, that something clicks in my head. And I suddenly realize, not consciously exactly, more as a physical sensation than anything else, that it's Lucky Richard all over again.

20

Red-haired Richie. Anything that can be done naked. Or half naked. Or with as little as a single member exposed. He has either done it. Seen it. Or heard about it. This according to his own account of things. One day he is going on about how he once copped a peek at his older sister's "bush." The next day he's telling us how he pilfered his brother's stash of *Playboys* and ogled all the centerfolds. He and his buddies. Another day it is the blow by blow of how he listened at the door while his mom and dad "went at it" one night.

Richard has always been full of this kind of talk. It's like a fever he has. A fever to which the rest of us have so far been generally immune. Perhaps because we have only ever regarded Richard as an amusing distraction at best. But that was before. Things have changed since then. Since the thing with Pee Wee and Walter. For those of us who had seen it, the shower room took on new dimensions when we came down for our morning routine. It was suddenly too small. Even though no one actually mentioned what had happened the night before. No one said much of anything. None of the usual restless chatter from any of us. Or horsing around. No splashing soap in the next guy's eyes. No snapping a towel at anyone's thigh. We averted our eyes. Not knowing just where to land them. An awkward modesty that had not been there before. When we fell out in front for the trek to breakfast, we side-eyed Walter when he walked out the door. Me looking to find some something. In his eyes. In his walk. In the pores of his skin. Some sign. Any sign. Of what, if anything, had been altered in him. But nothing met the eye.

We eyeballed Pee Wee too. On our way to the dining hall. Who strolled along. Charley at his side. As if nothing had happened. Me wondering if I was the only one putting two and two together. The only one thinking *Pee Wee and Charley, hmm. . . .* Not completely clear on what the *hmm* of it was exactly. Yet feeling a wave of envy over it. Not for the whole thing. Whatever that might entail. But for the closeness between them. As close, I imagined, as brothers at least.

Then everyone in the house finding out about it. No one quite sure, even as it was being whispered on to the next eager ear, what to say of Walter's part in it. After all, he had seemed bewildered as it was happening. Curious, rather than appalled. More interested in getting clear on what was going on than in wrestling or begging Pee Wee off him.

Victim? Pawn? Unwitting party to it all?

The jury was still out on that one.

The one thing we could all agree on. The one undeniable fact that managed to survive every telling of the tale. Was that Pee Wee had "got some." However makeshift his "getting some" had been. A coveted virtue among adolescent boys. And by which Pee Wee earned—was at the very least begrudged—a kind of ascension. For having danced near the flame.

The net effect of all this has been intensifying ever since. Our natural curiosity about whatever, besides peeing, can be done with the thing between our legs, grows ever more urgent. With each passing day. It isn't just Richie anymore. The fever has now caught us all.

Richie, however, remains its spokesman. I catch him and Marty and Bruce holding court in my old room one evening. When I go up to use the connecting bathroom. They give me guilty eyes as I walk through. And their voices drop into low register while I'm in there doing my business. I strain my ears. But I can't make out the words. When I step out again they hush up. Then, when I'm half through the doorway, one foot in the hall, Richie says, "Hey Stringer. Ya' ever masturbate?"

Masturbate. The first of several new, illicit words I will add to my vocabulary before the night is done. I like learning new words. I like especially when I can draw a bead on what they mean just from the way they sound. *Mast-ur-bate,* I repeat it in my head. And think of a big, fat, worm. A *master bait.* Dangling on a hook.

"He means," says Marty. In pajamas. Perched Indian-style on his bed. One hand grasping an ankle. "D'ya ever beat your meat?"

I just stand there. Absorbing that such business can be wrapped in such a fancy name. Then I'm afraid to answer. Not quite sure what is expected of me. Whether it is better to say that I have or that I haven't.

"It's the most natural thing in the world," Richie says. More to everyone than to me. "You beat your meat, don'tcha, Marty?"

Marty lets off a nervous laugh. His face going red. Richie looks at Bruce. He doesn't say a thing. The next thing you know, Richie's treating us to a step-by-step description of the art and rewards of pleasing yourself. *Boner* soon takes its place next to *masturbate* in my growing repertoire of new words. Modified by its more clinical variation, *erection.* Both of them sounds-like-what-they-mean words if I ever heard any.

". . . And after a while, maybe ten minutes or so, " Richie explains, "you get this kinda' thrill. Sorta' like an itch and a tickle both at the same time. And this gooey stuff comes out. Looks a little like spit and milk mixed together."

"Gross!" Marty says.

But he grabs a pillow. Places it over his lap.

"Ahh," Richie says. "It's clean stuff. Your seed. Your manhood. The stuff you make babies with. A sign that ya' reached your *puberty.*"

Four new words now. All in one sitting. I repeat this one, too, in my head. *Pu-ber-ty.* But get no clue at all from sounding it out. I glance at Marty. His eyes are on the floor. I glance at grownup-looking Bruce. Nothing. And none of us ask either. None of us wants to be caught not knowing. Not when it comes to anything to do with our "manhood" we don't.

I have to wait until school the next day to look it up. My teacher here got me into doing this. Mrs. Williams. I like her. Like her long, stringy hair. The way it is streaked with strands of gray in front. Like the one crooked and slightly yellow tooth she has. The way it seems to stand in protest of all the other pearly, perfectly even teeth lining the front of her mouth. Like the way she laughs. A throaty and genuine guffaw. Like how up front and straightforward she is about things. The way she laid out all that would be expected of us, the first day of class.

Somewhere in there she said something about *integrity.* A really neat word to my ears. And the way she used it, I got a good guess as to the drift of it. Figuring it had something to do with honesty. The kind that makes people trust you, more than the kind that keeps you out of jail. I threw my hand up anyway. Just to be sure. But Mrs. Williams wouldn't tell me squat. Just slapped a dictionary on my desk and told me to look it up. That's how she is with words. She never tells you. You always have to look it up.

I use the big dictionary. The one that sits on its own pedestal in the library. I look up all four new words. I don't find *boner.* Not in the same context, anyway. But the rest are there. And there are a bunch of definitions for *puberty.* One of them about plants first bearing fruit. The third entry, though, the *time of life when the sex glands become functional,* makes things clear enough. A revelation when put together with the rest. *Masturbate* and *erection* defining what had been expected, the evening Victor cornered my brother and me. *Puberty* explaining why it didn't happen. Leaving me to wonder, as I smile my way back past the librarian's desk, when my glands *will* be functioning. If they are functioning now.

21

Steve has pictures. Sexy pictures of cars. A big stack of brochures he has gotten from home. They are spread out at odd angles on his bed. He holds them at arm's length, one by one. Squints at them this way and that. It's Saturday. Nearly noon. All the other guys are outside playing and we're still at it. Still doing chores. A bitter pill, as far as I'm concerned. A thing to be dispensed with as expediently as possible. Steve, though, is slow and methodical about it. Is able to lose himself in mundane tasks.

"Whaddaya' think?" he says. He is holding a full-color glossy of a red and black Coupe DeVille flat against the wall. His fingers are long and even. Pale underneath and a touch of olive on top.

"Cool," I tell him.

It is hard to tell. He has an upper lip that is slightly upturned in that attitude anyway. But I think I detect the edge of a contented sort of smile on his face. As he neatly folds four pieces of scotch tape so that they are sticky on both sides. And places them squarely at the four corners on the back of the picture. I imagine him almost singing to himself. Steve loves clean and tidy. Each Saturday when we are finished and he steps back to take in how buff and trim everything is he is almost breathless in his delight.

"There," he chirps. Pressing the Coupe DeVille home. Amid the growing galaxy of slick machines already posted on his side of the room. He has car models too. On the shelf of the bay window in the middle of the room. A blue Chevy Impala and red Corvette Stingray he has built from Aurora car kits. Each cleverly perched atop a catalog picture of itself. My own side of the room looks threadbare by comparison.

He tries another picture against the wall. A GTO. With racing stripes along the sides. So sleek and muscular, it declares its own space up there. And gives me an idea. Downstairs in my footlocker I have a Daytona 500 racing set. Yet another gift from that glorious Christmas, years ago. When my father surprised us. It is no good for racing. The white car always runs faster than the other one so it is never a contest. But when I haul it upstairs and lay it out on the radiator cover just beneath the window it looks pretty good. Good enough to give Steve pause.

"Neat," he says, no mistaking that he is smiling now. His eyes go to my side of the room. Then find their way to me. "You want ta' put up any of these?" he adds with a wave toward his stash on the bed. A small courtesy, but it falls on me like profound kindness.

"Neat," I say.

A sudden burst of voices flutters up from outside. A softball game in progress. I have to fight off a tug when I see them through the window. Pounding around the softball field. And me in my room hanging pictures. Soon enough, though, I have another window to look through. A '62 Impala. Robin's egg blue, the caption says it is. Parked in front of a two-story suburban ranch house. With a lawn as vivid and even as carpeting. I fish this out of Steve's stash. Want to slap it right up on my side of the room. But manage to force myself to carefully tape the four corners and square it neatly on the wall above the head of my bed. The satisfaction is immense.

A dozen or so pictures later there's hardly any telling, anymore, where Steve's side of the room ends and my side of it begins. And the game outside is just an echo in my ear. We finish the last bit of the Saturday drudge. Wax and buff the floor. There is a creaky old Hoover buffing machine in the closet down the hall. But we use shine rags. Squares cut from old flannel blankets. Which we put under our feet. Then *ice skate* around the floor to work up a shine. When we are done, standing just outside the doorway, admiring our handiwork, Steve is so lit up, taking it in, his voice breaks.

"Our room looks really neat!" he squeaks.

Then he does something so totally unexpected my head reels. He hugs me. Both arms. Chest to chest. I hug back. My own neediness embarrassing me as I do. When we come to our senses and push back, Steve's face is flushed. Like sudden fever. He has to give me a little punch on the arm. To put the picture right again.

My mother has Wayne with her when she comes for her visit the next day. He is in his olive suit. The one he wears to church. It hangs like a sackcloth from his bony shoulders. I could tell him that shark-skin suits with stovepipe trousers are the big thing these days. Only Wayne couldn't care less about fashion or style. Standing there with that ethereal gaze a good hour or so of whooping it up with the Holy Ghost always brings to his face. He couldn't care less, it seems, about anything on and of this earth. I frown at him when he walks in the door. And try out the new word I have learned on the baseball field. Wish he were more cool. That he wasn't such a *doofus*.

Before they leave I bring the two of them upstairs. To show them the room. "Very nice," my mother says, beaming at the pictures on the walls. The stuff laid out on the radiator cover. The car models on the windowsill. Wayne is without comment. As he surveys the room. Eyebrows up. Precious little of his thoughts and feelings ever find their way to his lips. He plops down on Steve's bed before I can catch him.

"So who's your new roommate?" my mother wants to know.

"Steve," I tell her. Adding, "He's from the Bronx."

I don't know why.

When we get back downstairs I spot him with his mother. She is dressed in a liquid blue dress. It vibrates against the colors of her hair. Gold and rust and a hint of strawberry. Her lips are moist with gloss.

"Over there," I tell my mother. Motioning with my chin toward Steve. He is in a lemon shirt so pale it is practically white. And spotless white chino slacks that crease just so.

"That's him," I say.

It comes out sounding almost like a boast.

"Ah," my mother says, a near reverent look in her eyes. "I betcha *they* got money."

Later, after snacks, when we are in the TV room, I keep one eye cocked. To see what Steve will do. Thinking maybe we'd started being friends. And that there is no reason, now, for him to avoid me. He does his usual thing, though. Hauls himself from his spot on the floor about a half hour before lights out and heads out of the room for the stairs. A few minutes later I decide I want to write a letter home. That I have to go upstairs. To get a pencil. And some paper from my looseleaf binder.

The hallway is quiet when I reach the top of the stairs. There are no lights on in the room. A slight motion catches my eyes as I approach the doorway. A faint quivering of the bedspread. When I step in and snap on the lights, Steve starts. Quickly rolls over so that he is facing the wall. But he is not entirely quick enough.

I say nothing to him. Don't indicate in any way that I have seen a thing. Just continue to my locker. Retrieve my looseleaf. Snap off the light and go back downstairs. Then sit at the table in the TV room not writing anything. Tapping the blank sheet of paper in front of me with the eraser end of the pencil. Thinking, *so that's what it is. It isn't necessarily me after all. Who has driven him to bed early so many nights.*

My glossary of new words parades through my head. *Puberty. Masturbate. Boner.* And I picture Steve up there. Going at it with gusto. *Right hand or left?* And break into a prickly sweat. Suddenly jealous of his pleasure. When it's time for lights out and I get upstairs I find him asleep as usual. His eyes closed at least. I have my shiny new galaxy of pretty cars to welcome me. I'm still restless though. Can't seem to find a comfortable position in my bed. And turning first this way then that, I am fairly startled to discover that my glands are working after all.

22

Curiosity and urgency. Stalking our days. Troubling our nights. Only now in a less public way. Not so much a matter of salting up our idle talk. Or fueling our flights of fantasy. That still goes on some. Downstairs mostly. Upstairs, though, the heat is cooler. More intimate. The stakes are higher. More and more people come down the stairs and there is something new there. Some something just discovered up there. Deliberate, sometimes. The result of a one-handed voyage alone under the bedclothes. Or from more daring exploration. Done in tandem with someone else. But just as often it's the result of a chance encounter. Upstairs is full of secrets. You blunder into them along the halls. Fumble across them in the dark.

Something wakes me up one night. I go down the hall for a drink of water. Just as I'm settling back into bed I hear something outside the door. It is Louie. Loping down the stairs. Looking like he just rolled out of bed. He always looks that way. His eyes are heavy lidded. Always at least half closed. He never says much either. He is just there. And I sometimes find myself speculating about whatever could be on his mind.

He doesn't see me watching as he stops on the landing to tuck in the tail of his pajama top. The thing is, he is coming from the third floor. Which everyone knows is strictly off limits to us. Glenn, one of the relief counselors, lives up there. *What is Louie doing coming from there?* When he hits the landing just outside my doorway I have to close my eyes. A few seconds later I hear him. Hear the trickle of pee from the bathroom. And it comes to me. What is probably going on.

Another night during TV time I go upstairs. To use the bathroom. The one between my old room and the next. When I am finished and open the door and the light glares into the unlit outer room, Pee Wee is suddenly there. The bathroom light exploding off the whiteness of his pajamas. Creating the effect that he has suddenly materialized. I almost walk right into him.

"Pee Wee . . ." I say.

I have to look down to see his face, we are so close. It is tilted up. The eyes looking right into mine. Yet kind of half closed in attitude. A sleepy, bedroom look. And his lips are slightly parted. I can feel his breath just below my Adam's apple.

"Stringer . . ." he says. And stands right there. Still close. Head still tilted back. Arms hung at his sides. His breath coming quicker now. His eyes waiting like a dare. It is only a second or two that we are like this. But in that brief interval I know all that I need to know. Know what he is asking. The scent of it wafts off him. A picture of him and Walter in the toilet stall flashes through my mind. The way he had turned and grinned. How he stopped once we had all had a look. The whole thing a lark, as far as he was concerned. Nothing serious at all. Only he is not so casual now. There is a quiver of apprehension in his eyes. Of something he knows is at stake. It is the thing that causes me to blink. Find my way around him. Scurry down the hall.

Then it is me and Jay. The guy I play ping-pong with. Caught in the upstairs bathroom during chores. Both with our pants down. I don't know what on earth ever got into Mom Bedford. Barging in like that. Like she could smell out that there was something fleshy going on behind the bathroom door. She'd never done that before. I don't recall her even coming up the stairs during chores before. And I sure don't know what to make of what happened next.

Lucky for me I heard her just before she burst through the door. And had maybe half a second to spin around toward the sink. Giving her my back. And slip my zipper back up before she could see that it was open. Steve was stuck on the toilet. He must have gone red as a beet.

"What 'ave we hair, eh?" she said. Her accent goes twice as thick when she's all worked up. "Are you lads up ta?"

What we were up to was what any twelve-year-old boys might get up to. A serious game of *mine's bigger than yours*. One thing after another Jay and I had gotten onto the subject. And I wasn't going to put up with the *burnt-off* rap any more. I knew something about myself now. That at full throttle there is much more of me than meets the eye. A thing that could only be proven in the flesh. So there we were. *Diddling* our *puds*, as I have heard it called. To prove the point. What we were supposed to be doing was downstairs chores. It being winter. And no snow to bring on the outdoor stuff.

"I banged my tooth with the end of the mop doing the porch," I tell Mrs. Bedford. Tell her reflection in the mirror. "And ran up here to see if I chipped it."

Being a fast liar comes in handy.

"Aye," she says. Sounding like an old sailor. Then glances down at Jay. Sitting there. Elbows on his knees. Butt screwed into the toilet seat. Studying the floor tiles. While I start feeling around in my mouth. To make my story more convincing. *Jay will have to fend for himself.*

Three seconds go by before it strikes me what I've just done. That the hand that had been *down there* is now in my mouth. I manage to bang it on the medicine cabinet, I yank it out so fast. Then, in a perfect example of shutting the barn door after the cows have got out, as my mother would say, I turn on the water. Give both hands a quick blast of water. And towel them off.

"Well, back to work," I try, and head for the opposite door. Suddenly raking the yard seems like a terrific thing to be doing.

"And just ware d'ya think yore goin'?" Mom Bedford says. Standing in classic scolding mother pose, now. One hip wrenched to the side. Her hand on the other. I open my mouth. Expect another cool lie to leap to my lips. But nothing comes out.

"You call that washin' yore hands?" she says.

She strides over to the sink.

The hot water goes on full blast.

A cloud of steam makes for the ceiling.

"Ya' want ta' give yer hands a proper washin'," she lilts and seizes the bar of soap. Then, eyebrows angling in on the bridge of her nose, she proceeds to work up an awesome froth of lather. The soap becoming a live thing in her hands. Eeling back and forth between her fingers. As they slide, caress and ooze over each other.

"Thumb's th' busiest finger," she says, and begins kneading her thumb from heel to tip with her fist. In slow, rhythmic, up and down strokes. "Needs a good proper washin'," she sings into the billowing steam.

My eyes crawl over to Jay.

His eyes glide over to meet mine.

We both turn again to look at Mrs. Bedford. Who now seems to be off to some private place. It's as if Jay and I aren't even there. Up and down on the thumb, goes her sudsy pink fist. Excess froth falling off the tip and into the basin with each stroke. Moist, slithery, sucking sounds *boinking* and *gnushing* above the *hiss* of the tap. First one hand. Then the other.

Then, just as suddenly as she had begun, she kind of catches herself. Utters some half-embarrassed mumble. As she thrusts her hands under the gushing tap.

"The two of ya' oughtn't be mucking about up here," she says as she grabs a towel. And starts wringing her hands. Over and over again. Like someone with a soul full of sins to purge. Then catches herself again. Says, "Jolly well then. Better get on with yer chores." And she disappears down the stairs.

23

I've begun to halfways suspect that the *them* and *us* thing may not be the insurmountable divide it has always seemed to be. That it might even be that we all fit together in one way or another. And that it's just a matter of having enough time and opportunity to get around to recognizing this. Two things we have plenty of here. Time and opportunity.

I have noticed, for instance, that a kind of osmosis happens when people share a room. Each absorbing bits of the other. Like me. Picking up the way Steve tucks in his shirttail when he gets dressed. Methodically spading it into the waistband of his trousers. From front to back. With the flat of his hand. Instead of just shoving it in there like I used to do.

With Steve it's the way I talk. I learn about this one night. Finding him still awake for a change when I come up for lights out. And wanting to know where I ever got a name like Caverly.

"My mother," I tell him.

I kind of snap at him when I say it. I don't much like having such an odd name. Yet another degree of separation between me and everyone else. I regret it right away. My hostile tone. Which Steve picks up on. And clams right up. "It was the name of one of my mother's doctors," I explain. Adding that she liked it very much. And gave it to me when I was born. Steve says "*Oh*" to this. Then asks, in a tentative way, if I've ever had a nickname. I tell him no. Not any that were meant to be friendly anyway. He mulls this over for a while. Then says,

"What about *Cav?* I could call you *Cav.*"

I tell him sure. Liking it right away. Abashed, in fact, by the affection it conveys.

"Okay," he chirps. His voice the brightest I have ever heard it. "Then Cav it is!"

Someone down the hall yells *"Shaddup, you two."* And we do. Not wanting to bring Pop up the stairs. But I find the ensuing silence too thick.

"I didn't mean to snap at you like that," I whisper. Staring up at the ceiling. "Just that you caught me off guard. I mean you've hardly said *boo* to me since I've moved in here."

"It's okay," Steve says.

I hear him twist in his bed. Hear the sheets rustle.

"I-I'm not much of a talker, anyway," he adds after a bit. "I can never think of anything to say."

"I know what you mean," I say. Knowing just what he means. Yet surprised to hear it from him. If I had his looks. And could stand on the pitcher's mound firing bullets the way he can. I'd be in everybody's face. "Especially with some of these guys. Just waiting to pounce on anything you say. But you can't let that scare you off. Can't let that keep you from speaking your mind."

"I'm more of a listener. I like listening more," he decides. "Like when you talk. The words you use. Your voice."

"Yeah?" I say. Something leaping to the quick.

"Uh-huh," he says. "You always know what to say."

"Not really." I tell him. Shrugging it off. But everything except my lips is smiling. "It's just that I like to run my mouth. I can't help myself."

He giggles at this.

Who'd have thought it, I think to myself. *Steve, lucky son that he is, being shy and unsure of himself.*

A gradual process of osmosis.

And this surprise and that.

And next thing you know the two of us are at home with each other. More so even than with any of the other guys. I notice this when the cottage goes on a camping trip. A whole week upstate in the woods. And Steve and I are separated. Because it's three and four to a tent. Except for sleepy-eyed Louie and Glenn. The relief counselor from the third floor. They have the only two-man tent all to themselves. I get put in with three guys who are roommates. I'm like the uninvited guest who comes to stay.

Don't get me wrong. I love everything else about the trip. The musk of damp tarp in the morning. Eating hot dogs singed to perfection over the campfire. Ketchup drooling, like blood, over everything. Laying with my head sticking out of the tent at night, awed by the twinkling sky. And titillated by the chatter and cackle of unseen creatures in the dark. Fishing. Hiking. Exploring. Peeing against the trees! It's like one long, satisfying, primal scream. When it's over, though. And Steve and me plunk our outdoor gear down in the little room. It's like coming home.

There's a trip to Coney Island, too. The whole junior unit goes. I've never been before. But Coney Island has always loomed large in my mind. Ever since I saw *The Little Fugitive*s on TV. A movie about two boys left home alone. The older one to baby-sit his younger sibling. A bright, sunny day outside and he's stuck with looking after him. It makes me think of me and Wayne. How even though he has a year on me I kind of have to baby-sit him sometimes. So he doesn't get hurt like he always does.

To spice things up, the older brother plays a prank. Gives his little brother a rifle and then pretends, with a little ketchup, that he's been shot by him. The kid freaks out, thinking he's killed his brother, and runs away. Pretty hairy stuff. But the place he runs away to is Coney Island. And as soon as he's through the gate, the movie takes off on such a mesmerizing, endlessly magical journey. From the capricious to the macabre and, ultimately, to the sublime. You want to climb right into the screen. And you wish it will never end.

But eventually the sun falls low in the sky. And the older brother finally tracks him down. And when they slouch back home. To their cramped and gray apartment. And the unyielding rule of grownups. It's almost too sad to bear. A little like watching them march to their deaths.

I must have seen this movie half a dozen times. They show it all the time. Channel Eleven, I think it is. And I never get tired of watching it. It is like going off on a perfect trip. To some other, better world than this one. A paradise of wonder. A place in which anything and everything is possible. And when it's over I'm always left aching and lonely for hours.

It's the look on the boy's face when he finally finds his kid brother that does it. He's practically in tears. Mean as he was to him, he really loves the little snot. That gets me every time. My brother and mother may dream of heaven. I dream of Coney Island.

So I can hardly contain myself when the morning actually comes. And the doors of the bus swing open. Causing a bum's rush for the best seats. A thing that's all false starts for me. It's the "buddy system" for this trip. Meaning you find a friend to stick with for the afternoon. So that we don't all have to stay in one group. And each time I go to plop down in an empty seat, the guy in the next seat over says it's saved. For his buddy.

"What if you don't have a buddy," I finally ask.

"Then it's whoever you're sitting next to on the bus."

Then a fight breaks out. A shoving match really. Two guys scuffling over the window seat. And it brings one of the recreation counselors to the end of his rope.

"Uh-uh," he says. "I'm not having this! Not today!" He has to practically scream to get everyone's attention. "Now I'm going to count to three. And anyone not in a seat is getting off the bus."

It's enough for me. The mere threat of not going to Coney Island. I slam my butt down in the nearest empty seat. Empty for a good reason. Because it's right next to Swirtsky. Cry-baby Swirtsky, they call him.

Because he bawled himself to sleep every night his first week at Cottage Five. They also call him Pillsbury. After the Pillsbury Dough Boy. He kind of looks like him. Short and pudgy as he is. And he has that kind of whiny voice. Which he'll put on you at the drop of a hat. All the better to get under your skin. A thing he always seems determined to do. Especially if you're bigger than he is. Which is pretty much everyone when you get down to it. Five minutes of him in your face and even the more levelheaded guys want to bash his head in. I have to admit I don't get him. Bringing it on himself like that.

He refuses to even look at me when I sit down. Just pouts out the window. Watching them load the coolers of food and sodas in the luggage bay on the side of the bus. I start peering around. Debating which is worse. Risking being thrown off the bus for switching to another seat. Or being saddled with Swirtsky as my "buddy" all day. When I see Steve get on the bus.

"Steve!" I say.

"Hey," he says, adding, "Cav."

I love that name. Love being called this. He makes his way over to where I'm sitting. His expression inscrutable as ever.

"I-I thought they put you on the other bus," I say.

"Ahh," he says, "they asked me ta' help with the food."

He glances over at Swirtsky. Then back to me. And, true to his word about never knowing what to say, his lips come together. Then part again. Before he finally says.

"So, what, you wanna be buddies?"

It takes a doing to settle Swirtsky down. He doesn't want to move. And none of the other kids want him to sit with them. He whines. He pouts. He calls sleepy-eyed Louie a *faggot*, after Louie tells him to get lost. Finally, they tell him he can sit up front. With the grownups. And that does the trick. He hustles out of the seat. Mugging like a birthday boy. *Swirtsky.*

Who can figure him out?

It's off to Coney Island now. An infinity of bottles of beer on the wall happen to fall before we get there. An even more grinding thing once we have parked the bus. And have to go through the drill of being told where to meet up for lunch. And what time we have to return to the parking lot. Then the line-up to get our tickets. Which moves at a snail's crawl. My heart doesn't stop thumping through the whole ordeal.

Then it's me, Steve, Coney Island and a whole afternoon to ourselves. Hardly knowing where to start, we make a beeline for the hurricane coaster. I win a live goldfish on the way. In one of the games along the boardwalk. By tossing a ping-pong ball into its little bowl. I do it on the first try.

The whole day is like this. A day where anything and everything seems possible. It's just like in the movie. And at the end of it, when we are back on campus. And the sun is low on the horizon. And we are walking from the bus back to the cottage, eyes to the pavement, the same aching sadness descends. Both Steve and me trudging in silence. Then him looking over to me. And his eyes lighting up.

"So who's your best friend," he says.

I don't say anything. I'm all teeth. Can't wrap my lips around any words. I put a half-Nelson on him. Pull him into me. Give him a couple of noogies. Before he breaks away and I go chasing after him. Both of us belching laughter. As close and happy as brothers. The magic of summer coming through once again. Even in a place like this.

Then there's the next afternoon.

Steve and Andy choosing up sides for a softball game.

And Steve picks me.

"I'll take Cav," he says.

"*Stringer?*" Andy squawks. Like it's the dumbest thing that ever hit his ears. "You're taking *Stringer?*"

And Steve screws up the stuff to say it again.

"Yup. I'll take Cav," he says.

A thing Andy just can't get over.

"Well you can have him," he says.

He says this with a sneer. A sneer that I take with me to the plate every time I go up to bat. And which reappears on his face again and again. Each time I go down swinging. Which I do four times. All the more determined, each time, to murder the ball and wipe that smirk off his face. And each time all the more out in front of his lazy, meandering throws because of it. By the time I come up for the fifth time, my loathing for Andy is stinging the air between us like pinpricks. I can feel my fingernails dig into the wood of the bat. When he pops that cockeyed grin at me. And says, *"Easy out, guys. No hitter! No hitter!"* And my brain starts calculating the minimum number of seconds it would take to rush the mound. That I could be on him in a flash, with my speed. Before he even knows it's happening.

It's all I can do to hold myself back. I don't even think of swinging when he sends his first pitch up, I'm in such a pique. I just stand there and let it pass.

. . . It goes wide.

And the wattage of his grin dims down.

I decide to lay off the next pitch.

. . . It goes wide too.

Easily a ball.

"That's it, *Cav*," I hear. Steve. Cheering me on. "Wait for your pitch."

I step away from the plate. Bite back my anger at Andy. Shake off the miserable showing I've made with the bat so far. Then step back in. Just me and Andy and the bat and the ball, now. And nothing between one thing or the other but myself. Andy throws again. Eyes narrowed. Arm ramrod straight. Really wanting it over the plate. Practically handing the thing up to the catcher.

. . . It hits the dirt in front of me.

His worst toss yet.

Now a couple of my teammates chime in. I hear *"No pitcher! No pitcher!"* And, *"A walk is as good as a hit, Stringer!"*

It's a delicious noise.

Now I'm playing baseball! I tell myself. *Finally forcing Andy to pitch. And Andy being Andy, there is no way he'll get three in row over the plate. He just doesn't have the chops. All I have to do is wait him out.*

The fourth pitch seems to come at me in slow motion. I see Andy's pitching hand appear from behind his thigh. See his knees bend slightly. Then hoist his chunky frame upward as he releases the ball. I see the rotation on it as it nears. See, way before it is critical to see such a thing, that it is coming in too high. *A walk is as good as a hit,* I tell myself and crouch a little. Making a lower profile of myself. Even though I know it's not really necessary. That all I have to do is stand there and I will have won a trot down to first base.

Then, at the last possible second. Just as the ball is sailing up into my eyes. Just as I hear the catcher behind me scramble up from his crouch. Just as things have passed the point where a decision should have already been made. Something inside me nonetheless decides that reaching first by default is simply not enough. I feel my shoulders cock back. Feel my feet lunge forward. Feel the bat slice through the air. Feel a sweet punch quiver through my wrists. Hear the reassuring *thunk* of wood on the ball.

. . . That much of it is good.

The rest of it, though, is a dreadful mistake.

I am way out in front of the thing again.

"Easy out," Andy says again. As the ball skips lamely but surely toward the third baseman. Who lazily dips his mitt. And it is a point of departure for me. I am not willing to let it go at that. I simply refuse to let it happen. In the next tenth of a second I'm no longer in the batter's box. I'm blistering down the first base line. Oblivious to everything except that little canvas square at the end of it.

This catches everyone by surprise.

Not least of whom, the third baseman.

Who hustles to recover. Bare-hands the ball. And tosses it off to first while still on the run. A rocket of a shot. But it veers off line. The first baseman has to more than stretch to grab the thing. It pulls him up and off the bag. By the time his feet hit ground again I'm already blazing toward second. Ignoring the groans I hear as I make the turn. Ignoring my teammates' attempts to shout me back. Ignoring the odds against my ever outrunning the throw. Pounding down the second-base line with all that I have in me.

I hit the dirt three paces off . . .

Go into second head-first . . .

Careen into the second baseman's legs . . .

He cascades down on top of me. Elbows and knees landing like punches to my back and ribs. But I hug the bag like it's a long lost lover. And gasping for breath, every gulp of it also a stab in my side, I open my eyes. And see the ball. Mere inches from my nose. Laying on the ground like an unwanted orphan. *I'm safe! Safe on second base!*

I hear *"Way to go, Stringer! Way to go!"* as I lift myself up and dust the dirt off. I hear *"Bring him home, baby. Bring him home!"* as the next batter steps up. But for me it isn't about making it home. Or scoring a run. Or even winning the game. I am beyond baseball now. Had been since the moment I decided to go for it. From the second I dropped the bat, it was no longer about beating the throw. Or outrunning the ball. It was about wanting to declare war on the very idea of impossibility.

24

I think it's stepping back from the fray. Giving yourself a chance to focus a little before you act makes a big difference. Gives you a whole new perspective on things. Not just on the softball field, but in all kinds of situations. Like when I go home overnight in early August. After eleven months being away. A big difference, I discover, between living there and being there as a guest. Everyone in the house treating me like a celebrity or something. So anxious that I am comfortable and happy. Everyone except maybe Wayne, that is. Who has had our room all to himself all this time. When I plop my overnight things on the bed it's like I'm invading his private domain.

But the rest of the weekend is all me. For dinner we have one of my favorite dishes. Shrimp and rice. The way my mother makes it. With egg and peppers and who knows what other tasty things stirred into the fry. And homemade lemon meringue pie for dessert. When the TV goes on, I get to pick what I want to see. I watch *Saturday Night Wrestling, The Fugitive* and *The Twilight Zone.* I'm even allowed to stay up late. To see a little of *The Tonight Show.* Which I've only ever heard before through the living room door. An utterly beguiling thing to actually see. A roomful of grownups. Gathered at the edge of the night. For the sole purpose of laughing it up and having fun.

Sunday morning no one comes to wake me up. I sleep in for as long as I want. And since Wayne is almost thirteen now, able to make the trek to church on his own, my mother stays home to make a special late breakfast just for me. I wake up to the smell of coffee. Wafting from the living room. Brewed coffee. Not the instant stuff we usually have. When I go out to the living room I see the card table set up in front of the big picture window. See the good plates and silverware laid out. The ones reserved for special occasions. And seeing what's for breakfast, I have a giddy giggle. Bagels and lox with cream cheese. Marty gave me my first taste of this stuff after visiting hours one Sunday. And I asked my mother if she could bring some up.

"Salmon!?" she had said. "Do you know what that costs? That's rich people's food."

Which thrilled me all the more. And thrills me now. To see it laid out on the table. As if we are, for the moment at least, rich. Rich, that is to say, in the sense that I've always imagined it. That there are no such words as *can't* and *no.* Two words that seem far away right now. The two of us sitting there in front of the big picture window. A feast of food laid out before us. And then there it is. My mother's smile. It reaches across the table as she pours me a cup of coffee. Her face bathed in late morning sunshine. It sparkles in the moment. Sparkles on the plates and silverware. Blazes off the chrome of the coffee pot as she pours. A blinding flash. Like a light straight from heaven. It has nothing to do with anything, really. Yet I'm baptized in its brilliance. A calm and contentment I've never known. A moment of utter peace with my mother I will remember with precision forever.

When it is time to go, my mother tucks the cab fare in my shirt pocket. And puts me on the bus. I feel a tug that was not there when I was first shipped off to sleepaway school. And when the bus starts to pull away and I see them. My mother and brother. Both of them smiling. Their faces receding. The impulse is to leap up from my seat. A thing that I would do: Tell the driver *Stop the bus!* Step back off and run to them. Forget all about sleepaway school. If only it could be like this all the time.

Then there is Michael. Meeting his father. I go right over there my first day home. And find a man standing on his little square of a porch. Wrapped in a terrycloth bathrobe. Even though it's nearly noon. He nods *hello* when he sees me. And I ask if Michael's home.

"He's out with his mother," he says through the corners of his teeth. Munching away on something. "Should be back in a little while. Half hour or so."

What he's eating, I notice as he's telling me this, is a hot dog. A *raw* hot dog. I see the package in his hand.

"Don't you have to cook that?" I want to know.

"What, and cook all the 'trition out the thing?" he snorts. His face crinkles. Into a scolding frown. "Shoot, boy. Don't know what choo talking 'bout." He follows this with a *Hrrmph* sort of sound. Chews off another hefty chunk of the link in his hand. And moves it around in his mouth. Does this with such relish, I half want to go right home and have one myself.

"You ever taste one fresh out the package, boy?" he says.

I tell him no.

"Course not!" he booms. So loud and sudden I jump when he says it. "'Swhy you're talking out your mouth."

He holds out the package.

"Show you what's good," he says. Manipulating a frank through the wrapping. Until it's halfway out the opening. I just stand there. Looking at the thing. "Go ahead, now," he says. "Won't kill ya."

It's not what my mother tells me. But curiosity gets the better of me. I take the thing. Like a man taking an offered cigar. Then nibble the end off. Just like it is a cigar. And give it a few tentative bites. It doesn't taste half bad.

"What'd I tell ya," he says. His grin revealing a missing tooth.

We stand there for a while. Both munching away. Not saying anything. I can hear cicadas rasping. From the lot across the street. Just background noise to me before. But a familiar and comforting music now. Before I know it the frank I'm eating is gone. A satisfying thing. Like I've just accomplished something grownup. So satisfying I'm ready to hang right there until Michael shows.

But a minute later I'm dismissed.

Told to run along.

"I'll tell Michael you were here," he says.

Later, when Michael rings my bell. And I open the door and see him there. I start grinning. "I met your father!" I tell him. Envious of him. That his father has come home. "He gave me a hot dog. It was good."

Michael runs a knuckle under his nose. And drops his eyes.

"He drinks," he tells me. "My mother doesn't like having him around. They argue and fight." He says this with a quiet sadness. Which I only now realize, after knowing him all this time, is always with him.

Then there's Swirtsky. Of all people. Seeing even him in a different way. During summer's last hurrah. A five-day spree of team and individual competition. The Maccabeah. Named after the man, I'm told, who waged gallant and glorious battle, years ago. During something called the *Color Wars*. And in which tradition the junior unit has been divided into three teams. Red, gold and my team. The color I draw from the hat when it's my turn to pick. The blue team. Which means it's blue shorts for me. And a white t-shirt with a blue shield imprinted on the breast. There's a blue-team banner, too. And even a blue-team song:

Hoo-ray for the blue . . .

That's the team for you . . .

The blue team is the best . . .

Just put us to the test . . .

. . . And so on. Sung to the tune of *Ta Rah Rah Boomdeeay.* And it's me who makes it up. Seems I have a knack for concocting rhymes. It just falls out of my mouth when the question of a team song comes up. It takes first prize when we present it on the opening day. Twenty-five points for the team. I have my chest out to here all day. I take first place in the javelin throw, too. Even though I never threw a javelin before. And when Steve and I happen to get paired up in the three-legged race, where they tie your right leg to someone else's left and you have to run like that, we clear the finish line way before the pack. We don't stumble once. It's as if we are one person.

So by Friday morning, the last day of the thing, I'm on top of the world. With five ribbons. Three for first place and two for second. More than a hundred points in all for the blue team. Which is neck and neck with the gold to win the whole thing. And me being part of it all.

I'm out on the porch. Trying to sort out all the junk I've built up in my footlocker. When Swirtsky walks in. And right away you can see he doesn't know what to do with himself. Swirtsky being Swirtsky, that usually means trouble. I try ignoring him. As if he isn't even there. But he's not to be ignored when he doesn't want to be. He starts out with pesky little questions. *"Where'd you get that thing? God. Do they still make those?"* Commenting on everything I pull out of my footlocker. When no one asked his opinion in the first place. Then it's all about this thing being cheap and that thing being broken and the other thing being tacky. I try shrugging him off. But I'm telling you, Swirtsky's like a bee buzzing in your face. He's got being annoying down to a science. And, one thing after another, I call him a name. *Shitface*, I call him, the word *doody* now permanently purged from my vocabulary.

"Why don't you shut up, shitface," I say.

That's when he decides to call me a name back.

And the name he chooses to call me is *nigger.*

"Why don't you go back to Africa, you nigger," he says.

My mother has talked to me about this kind of thing. The people at Central School, too. Practically every grownup I know, in fact. And they always tell me the same thing. About sticks and stones breaking your bones. But that words can never hurt you. That and the thing about turning the other cheek. And the one time it had happened before that's what I did. It was on the school playground. A white kid. Real white. Pale as a ghost. So striking, you couldn't help but notice him. With trim and tidy features. Aligned in perfect symmetry. Even the lines of his hair. As if an artist had lovingly sculpted him out of alabaster.

"'Choo looking at," he sneered. The corner of his lip almost reaching his nose. "Fuckin' nigger."

I did as I was told. Turned the other cheek and walked away. But the grownups had it wrong about words. About this one at least. Venom. Contempt. And loathing. From a perfect stranger. An entirely potent word. Strong enough to ugly up even this kid's pretty face. It more than hurt. It was downright heartbreaking. I felt sick and miserable inside for days afterward.

With Swirtsky though it just pisses me off. That a squirt like him would have the bald gall to throw a word like that in my face. And even so, I turn as much of a cheek as I can. I do give him a shove. A rude one at that. The palms of both my hands careening into his shoulders and knocking him down. But I don't do half of what I feel like doing to him. Don't touch his face. Or punch him. Or anything like that. And the shove I give him should only back him up. Isn't really enough to hurt him. But he splats down anyway. Lands on that fat butt of his and starts shrieking. A piercing, wounded wail that could cut through stone. Not only is it out of all proportion to what's happening, there's something deliberate and practiced in the way he delivers it.

Then it strikes me. That what I'm watching is not what it looks like. It's not Swirtsky crying out in pain. It's Swirtsky sending out an alarm. And sure enough, five seconds later here come Mom and Pop. Right on cue. Out to the porch on a run. And the first thing to hit their eyes is the tableau Swirtsky has so deftly engineered. Him, the defenseless little curly-haired boy. On the floor in tears. And me. The brute. A guy twice his size. Looming over him. I almost want to laugh, watching Mrs. Bedford rush to Swirtsky. Watching Swirtsky fold himself into her matronly arms, collecting his miserable prize.

Then there's Pop. Leaping into his assigned role. Putting himself between Swirtsky and me. Barking spittle into my face. Promising to let me have the back of his hand, boy! A threat that has lost its iron, after hearing it so many times.

But it's the powerlessness I feel. Knowing they'd both just been had by Swirtsky. And that there is nothing I can do about it. Nothing I can say that will alter a thing. Since there is something in it for everyone concerned. Except me. And this is what sends hot lava singing through my brain. Knowing I'm merely a pawn in their happy business.

It's one, two, three after that.

One, me telling Pop how he can to go to hell.

Two, Pop actually doing it.

Giving me the back of his hand.

A backwards and bony slap that clips the side of my face.

And three, me spinning around. Going straight for the door. Knowing I'll start splashing blind fury all over the place if I stay another second. Then slamming the door too hard behind me. The glass pane shattering under the force.

One. Two. Three.

A trio of sharp notes.

Slap! Bang! Crash!

25

If I peer through the base of the trees, I can see the edge of the blacktop. Where it curves around toward the AB building. Can see people heading for the dining hall. It must be after five. By now they probably have me down for AWOL. Which is army talk for running away. And I can't say I didn't have half a notion to do just that when I stormed off this morning. But I came down here. To my secret place. A dark and quiet spot amid the pine trees. That's one thing about this campus. It's ringed all around by a dense and fragrant perimeter of bushy Douglas firs. That have carpeted the ground with their pine needles. It's pretty peaceful. Being in here all by yourself. Free to think as you wish. No matter what. Your most private thoughts. And there is no one to get on you.

Sometimes, when everybody else is busy doing other stuff, I'll disappear into the pines and just sit here. Sometimes I even talk out loud about stuff here. I can't say it solves everything, doing that. But I usually feel better afterward. As if I have been heard. As if there were a friendly ear hiding out here somewhere. A listener in the pines.

So here I came. When it hit the fan with Swirtsky and Pop this morning. And right away some of the steam oozed out of me. I thought, *run away to where?* Not home. My mother would only turn me around and bring me right back here. That's if I could find my way there in the first place. I'm not like Wayne. Who must be part homing pigeon. Plop him down in the middle of nowhere and he'll navigate his way right back to our front door. Not me. Get me a couple dozen blocks out and I might as well be in China.

Besides which, truth be told, I don't really want to leave. Not now. Not on the last day of the Maccabeah. Not when I've just begun to matter. And they are coming around with me. The other kids here. Starting to treat me like one of the gang. Not when I'm starting to halfways think there just might be a way around this angry mess I've been in for so long. Even if I don't quite know what that way is yet. And certainly not after this summer. Pee Wee had been right after all. Though not exactly in the way he meant it. I've never had it quite this good. This has been my best summer yet. I've actually been full of happiness. Even though I'm here.

Then I thought about Swirtsky. Even felt a little sorry for the little nudge. It's a pretty sad business when you get right down to it. Trawling for crumbs from grownups the way he does. A hug. A pat on the shoulder. A few consoling words. He has to be the neediest lucky son I know. Imagine his parents. Sending him here. When what he craves most is theirs to give him.

Then I cried.

A long, solemn weep.

For all the loneliness there is.

For the world being the way it is.

I have to tell you it felt good. And I haven't cried since without there being a little ray of joy right behind it. For all the bad stuff I know I'm finally letting go of. I headed for the recreation field after that. For the last of the Maccabeah. And was able to slip into the queue after Pop dropped the boys off. None of the rec guys knew a thing. The blue team didn't win. Gold nosed us out by a hair. But it was plenty of fun all the same. Knowing I was there on the sly.

It won't do to go to dinner in my blue team get-up, though. Not on a Friday night. I sneak into the empty cottage. Through the back of the house. Wince at the sight of the boarded-up porch door. Hustle up the stairs. Before I even clear them I get a shock. Like a clap of thunder and a right cross. Both at the same time. Even from the hallway I can see it. On my side of the room everything is bare. The sill of the bay window. The top of the radiator cover. Stripped. None of my stuff is there. Not even Mikey. My goldfish and his little bowl. Whom I named after Michael back home. The walls on my side, too. Ravaged. All the pictures are gone.

I don't shower. Or polish my shoes. Or bother with my hair. Just get dressed. In a daze. When I get to the dining hall they're already clearing the middle table away. I go straight to the alcove and present myself.

"So, you're back, eh?" Mrs. Bedford scowls.

I put my eyes to the floor. Flex my clodhoppered toes.

"I-I never left," I tell her. "I was here all day. On campus. At the Maccabeah. Really. You can ask the guys."

She lets out what starts as a sigh but finishes off as a *hrrmph.* I force myself to look at Pop. Standing at the head of the table now. Ropy arms at his sides. Bushy eyebrows up. Making a hard and curious study of me. As if I were a stranger to him.

"Might as well 'ave your supper then," Mom Bedford says begrudgingly. Quickly adding, "But then it's off with you to see the OD straight away when ya' finish."

She sings this. As if settling the details of a happy social event. We line up to get our food. Me doing my best to keep my eyes averted. It's such a public thing. Getting yourself jammed up here. Everyone side-eyeing you. That *better you than me* look stabbing at you again and again. I study Nathan. Dark and wiry. With fierce, arresting, intelligent eyes. And handsome, chiseled features. Garnishing every plate with a dollop of suppressed contempt before he slaps it down. A prince, perhaps, in some other time or place. But a misspent menial here.

And Mr. Travis. Who never misses a Friday night. Is always standing at the helm. Hands on his hips. Eyes counting off each disappearing plate. Face rage-red as always. His mouth twisted in. As usual. Forever straining against the scorn that wants to leap to his lips. The look of a man for whom few things ever meet with his approval.

I told him he fed us "like Greek gods" once. The morning I got back from my home visit. We were all lined up for breakfast. And he was behind the counter. Perusing the sports pages of the *Post.* Which he lowered the slightest hair.

"That so?" he said. His eyes drilling into mine.

"Yup," I replied, springing the quip I heard Alan King come out with on *The Tonight Show* the night before. "You give us burnt offerings every morning."

His eyes closed down to little slits when I said it. And for a moment I thought he was going to leap across the steam table and pounce on me. Beat me within an inch of my life, as my mother would say. Instead he just fried me to a crisp with his burning eyes. But the one-liner got me a good laugh from the guys. Even a slap on the back from one. I've made a habit of cracking wise at the food ever since. Even though it's not so bad.

I keep my trap shut tonight, though. Not needing to bring any more trouble on myself than I already have. And Mr. Travis nods at me. Suspiciously. Realizing I'm watching him. Keeps his eyes on me all the way down the line. A look that says *okay wiseass, let's hear it.* I drop my gaze. Gather my plate. Make for the alcove without a peep. And halfway between here and there it just dawns on me. Like two and two coming together. Why Mr. Travis is never not here on Friday night. Friday is fried chicken night. The best meal of the week. Who'd have thought it, the miserable grouch. It's pride that has him standing there.

I'm still kind of grinning over this discovery when I sit down in my usual spot. And I guess it gets to Mrs. Bedford. Because she jumps up from the table. Marches over to where I'm sitting. Snatches my plate right from under my hovering fork.

"You aren't fit ta' eat with the rest of us," she says. And walks my plate to the far corner of the alcove. To the "slop table." Where we keep the bucket we scrape what's left on our plates into after we're finished. It's never entirely clean. Always spotted with bits of moldy, caked-on food. Always stinks. Like moldering cheese.

"You can jolly well eat here," she sings. And plops my plate down there. Inches away from the drooling bucket. "Till ya learn ta' behave yourself like decent people."

A side of her I've never seen before. I glance over at Pop Bedford, settling into his chair. Any disciplining that has had to be done has always been left to him. He doesn't say anything. Doesn't even look my way. Just unfolds his napkin. Sets it on his lap. And begins to eat.

Everyone else is gaping at me. Still standing, shell-shocked, by the slop table. All those fresh-scrubbed, slicked-back faces. Giving me that sorry look you save for the damned. And while all I've wanted to do since the whole Swirtsky thing happened is put it behind me, take my lumps and move on, the consequences of it just keep piling up. First the room and now this. It's too much for me to hold in. Every nerve in me starts firing off rounds. I watch my hand seize the plate. Lift it from the table. High into the air. And send it slamming into the slop bucket so hard it smashes into pieces.

Everyone stops eating. Mom Bedford's jaw drops open. Pop leaps to his feet, the "back of his hand" already flying upward. And I give him the dare. Stand there and wait for the blow. It never comes. I step out of the alcove. March through the dining hall doors. Eyes straight ahead.

Mrs. Bedford stalks after me.

"You kin run if ya' want," she hollers. Standing in the doorway.

I keep walking.

"I'll have the OD after ya' in five minutes!" She says.

She goes back inside. I hear the door swing shut. And realize I have been holding my breath. I take a deep drink of the outside air. It's just right. Cool, clean, perfumed by the musk of summer. My eyes sail over to the AB building across the way. To the lights still burning in one first-floor window. Dumphy would be in there right now. His ear to the phone. And I can only imagine what Mom Bedford is telling him. *Stringer has gone mad again! He just ran completely amok in the dining hall.*

The corridor is dark and deserted when I step inside the AB building. My footsteps echo back to me. A spooky, dungeon feeling. My hand is unsteady when I finally screw up the courage to knock on Dumphy's door.

"Yes," I hear from the other side of it. "Come in!"

Dumphy's behind his desk. A lit gooseneck lamp between him and me. The low-angle glow hollows up his eyes. Gives him an evil, Nosferatu look. He gets to his feet when he sees me. His nose lit up. Bushy eyebrows scrunched in. His gray, double-breasted suit strains around the waist. A barrel of bone-crushing beef under there.

"Just who the hell do you think you are?" he roars. Stepping around the desk. Coming right up on me. "King shit?!" I get just a blurred glimpse of his huge right paw. As it arches down and explodes against my face. Then a bright burst of stars. The room tilts. The floor coming up to meet me. Until I find myself staring up at the ceiling. My right cheek burning like acid has been poured on it. My eyes and nose beginning to flood. It's the last thing on earth I want to do right now. Cry in front of Dumphy. But I can't stop myself.

"Hit me all you want," I hear myself say. A moan really, that verges on a sob. "But anybody calls me a nigger I'm gonna do the same thing."

I don't know where this comes from. I am nowhere near as brave or sure as my words. Soon as I get it out it I'm terrified. That I have said such a thing.

"Who called you that, son?" Dumphy scowls. "Who says you're a nigger?"

"And I didn't hit him. Just gave him a little push. It was nothing."

Dumphy sighs. Easing the strain off the double row of buttons on his jacket. "Well, Jesus, Joseph and Mary," he mutters. And glances out the window. "No one said anything about all that."

"I hardly even touched him. I just pushed him a little, that's all. For calling me that." I'm sobbing now. Just what I don't want to do.

"All right, son," Dumphy says. In a voice so quiet and gentle that if it wasn't just him and me in the room I would swear someone else had spoken. "C'mon now lad, pick yourself up."

He is just a step away from me when he says this. His arms poised stiffly at his side. As if he is about to extend a helping hand. But something holds him back.

I get to my feet, but still keep my distance. And Dumphy's hand rises again. Disappears inside his jacket. And emerges with a fluffy, white handkerchief. It looks ridiculously dainty. Dangling from his thick, stubby fingers. I take the thing and put it to my face. More to cover up my sniffling than to mop the snot from my upper lip.

"There you go," Dumphy says, moving to the door. "You go on back to your cottage now." I step through, into the empty hallway. Hand him back the handkerchief. Dazed and a bit confused. "I'll take care of this," he says. "And anyone else says that to you," he adds, the gruff edge back in his voice now, "you come see me."

26

I don't go back to the dining hall. I go to my spot. On a tide of giddiness. Having escaped Dumphy's full wrath. But once I'm amid the quiet and cover of the trees, my thoughts keep going back and forth. First there's Swirtsky. How he had pulled the *n* word out of his bag of tricks. Utterly certain that in springing it I would dance at the end of his string. Then there's Dumphy. With his blood-simple, ex-cop's, knee-jerk certainty as to just where the lines between right and wrong are indelibly drawn. Letting me off the hook like that. Back and forth between these two poles. Until my elation sours. And I wander back up from the pines. Feeling bothered and unsatisfied. Knowing, as I meander back to the cottage, that the Bedfords weren't the only ones who'd played straight into Swirtsky's hands. Dumphy's verdict notwithstanding, I can't quite let myself off the hook for that.

I find Mrs. Bedford waiting for me in the foyer. Mr. Dumphy must have called ahead to let her know he had sent me on my way. "There you are," she huffs when I walk through the door. I see a box of Hershey bars in her hand and glance at the clock on the wall. Alarmed. *Have I been that long? Is it snack time already?* But no, the clock tells me, it's just before seven. Snack time isn't until around seven-thirty. She regards me for a minute. A long, *whatever am I going to do with the likes of you* appraisal. And sighs. A low, drawn, beast-of-burden lament. Then opens the box of Hershey bars. And, eyes still on me, strides into the TV room.

I watch from the foyer. Everyone clustering around her like livestock at feeding time. Doling out to her chickens. To everyone but me, of course. I "don't deserve" to have snacks, she proclaims aloud. As she parcels out the treats to everyone else. Adding that, as of now, I am on dep "indefinitely." No snacks for me. No TV. No rec time. No privileges of any kind.

"We don't behave like wild hooligans around here," she says. Her eye cocked my way as she says it. Because of my "unacceptable behavior," she says, I am "not fit" to be a part of the group. Therefore until further notice no one is allowed to play with me. Or associate with me in any way. Anyone caught so much as speaking to me, she says, will be put on dep as well.

She puts the lid back on the box of Hersheys after announcing this. Anyone up or downstairs notwithstanding. And steps back into her apartment. Leaving me to face a roomful of silent sorry stares. And for a moment I teeter on the edge. Wanting to lash out at something. Tear. Crush. Squash. Upend tables. Put my foot through the TV screen. Kick the living shit out of anyone or anything within reach. Instead, I don't know why, I turn and climb the stairs to my room.

When I get there, though, I am reminded of my missing things. And stumble back downstairs. To the back porch. Flip open my footlocker. Thinking they must have put my stuff there. But that too is empty. Everything is gone. Not just the stuff that had been upstairs. Run back upstairs, panic rising, and peek in the TV room. There is no sign of Mom or Pop. Just the guys. Whiling away the quiet of the evening. Watching TV. Playing cards. Tinkering with their model kits. Their serenity appalls me.

I race back out to the foyer. To Mom and Pop's apartment door. Give it a couple of tentative knocks. No one answers. There is just the sound of their chattering TV. I knock again. Louder this time. Knowing, now, this was all Mrs. Bedford's doing. And hearing footsteps approach, hope it will be Pop who comes to the door. But it's *her.* She cracks the door open and sticks her head out. She is chewing something. This appalls me, too; I don't know why.

"Yes?" She says.

"My stuff," I stutter. "It's not there. My footlocker's empty!"

She dispenses with her cud in a trio of rapid chews and one wholesale swallow. I hear the juices squeeze themselves down her throat.

"Oh, that rubbish," she says with a wave of her hand. "... Clutterin' up the place. I threw the lot of it in the trash."

My mouth falls open. But nothing comes out. I back away from her. Head for the front door. "Where do you think you're—" is all I hear before the door closes on her bother. I go to the garbage bin. Fish through the trash inside. Until the violence of what I see halts my hand. There's my stuff all right. In the trash. Except that each and every item has been smashed or crushed. And every picture has been torn to bits. *This isn't happening!* ... I kick the can. Storm back and forth. Peer at the cottage. Kick the can again. There is nothing I can even conceive of doing that will come close to satisfying the wholesale outrage coursing through me. No one to whom I can appeal the enormity of what has been done.

I slump back up to the ravaged room. Drop down on the bed without turning on the lights. But I can still *feel* my missing things. Even in the dusk. For a good twenty minutes I sit there. Fuming. Wanting to cry. But preferring to ward off feeling sorry for myself by clinging to rage. And then, most peculiarly, I feel a subtle, warming sensation impose itself. Something unwanted. That makes no sense at all to me. That I am loath to let myself consciously admit. What I am feeling, inexplicably, is a sense of ... *satisfaction.*

I lay there staring at the ceiling until it is nearly time for lights out. Watch Steve drag himself up the stairs. He has a distracted, lazy drawl of a walk at the end of the day. Which always makes me wonder what might be piping through his mind. Watch him, embarrassed by the fondness I feel. As he steps to his locker. Removes his robe. Drapes it neatly on a hanger. All without a word or eye my way. Then peels back his bedclothes and wiggles himself beneath them.

Pop makes his rounds from room to room. Stops to study me for a moment before he snaps off the light. I want to ask him what he thinks about all that's going on. Then realize that I don't want to risk finding out that maybe he was in on it, too. I just watch him snap off the light and go downstairs. Then glance across the room.

"Steve . . ." He's lying on his side. Facing the wall. His back to me. I put my eyes back on the ceiling. "They threw out my stuff," I try. And hear a rustling of sheets from his side of the room.

"Steve?" I say. And hear more rustling. A hint of annoyance in it now.

"You heard what Mom said," he rasps. And I picture him. His lips pouting when he says it. "We're not supposed to talk to you."

"Who the hell's gonna know?" I tell him with weakening hope. That he will perform this one, small duty of friendship.

"Will ya' lemme go ta' sleep," he snaps.

I wake up cross and uncertain the next morning. We walk to breakfast. No one saying boo to me. I wrap the silence around me like a wall. Take refuge in the *them* and *me* of it. Stalk to the steam table when we get there. Take my plate to the alcove and sit in my regular seat. Ready for it now. Ready for Mom Bedford to say something, now. *Wanting* her to just try making me sit at the slop table.

She takes notice, when she comes into the alcove. And I don't miss it. The little hitch in her step. Her jaw goes taut, too, as she settles her plate at the head of the table. She looks away as she takes her seat. Leaves me to smolder in the anger I've been stoking since I got out of bed. I pick at my eggs. Chase the cereal around the bowl with my spoon. Steal glances at Pop every now and then. Confused at how passive he has been in all this. He sees me looking. Never lets his eyes settle on mine.

Mostly, I watch Mrs. Bedford. Taking her food in small, ladylike mouthfuls. Her chew is tightlipped, but fairly rigorous. It is clear how much she wants her food. However vague her expression may be in conveying any enjoyment of it while she eats. I notice her nose. How severe and stingy the nostrils are. Notice the strands of black hair. Which flare out from the openings. *A witch,* I tell myself. Nothing less than sorcery. How precise and perfect the hell she has calculated for me.

I notice her hands. Follow the dance of her tiny, tapered, fingers. The same fingers that had wrestled against one another so obscenely in an orgy of suds. That afternoon in the upstairs bathroom. They seem vulnerable somehow now. As they handle the fork. Tear at a crust of toast. Serve her mouth. An intimate business. All too intimate. I have to pull my eyes away.

I complain to Mrs. Mendelsohn. During my session with her the next day. Tell her everything that has happened. Pour it all out in a gush. She listens closely. As level and removed and professional as ever. Asks a clarifying question or two. Never gives me the sense of outrage I want from her. Only wants to know how I feel about it.

"I won't go back to the cottage," I tell her. "She hates me. I'm not going back. I'll go AWOL first."

But you can't run stuff like this on Mrs. Mendelsohn without her doubling it back on you.

"Why do you feel everyone hates you?" she says. Leaning forward in her chair.

And I want to yell.

Haven't you heard a word I've been saying!

But don't.

I just twist up another notch and say nothing.

"I can't help you if you don't talk to me," she says.

It feels like we're going in circles.

"What's there to talk about?" I tell her. "I already *told* you what happened. All my stuff. My property. Gone! Can't you just do something? Call someone? It isn't fair. What's sitting here talking about it going to do?"

She tells me she has no authority to tell cottage parents what they should or shouldn't do. "It's not my place to undermine their authority," is how she puts it. "You can understand that, can't you?"

I tell her "Yes." I understand.

But only to let her off the hook.

Two days later my consignment to leper status is suddenly lifted. I'm no longer even on dep. A development for which I give Mrs. Mendelsohn the credit. Despite what she had told me. Nothing, though, is said or done about my trashed possessions. I find my way to letting Steve off the hook too.

"Great!" he squeaks. When I tell him it's over. "We can be *friends* again, now!"

I act as if there's been no betrayal. Being too fascinated by him. By the fact that he, lucky son that he is, has befriended the likes of me at all.

27

A week before school resumes both Louie and Glenn disappear. One day they are there, and then on the next they are not. There is no official explanation given. No hint of where they have gone. Just an announcement that Glenn has resigned. That Louie has been transferred. But most of us know the score.

Glenn is quickly replaced. By Burl Gomillion. Crew cut. And half a shade lighter than me. Built like a linebacker, too. So muscled, it is almost obscene to look at him. No matter what he wears. The bulge of his biceps and the sharp *V* of his torso show right through his clothes. The very opposite of Glenn. Who was slight and bespeckled. With a needle nose. And limp, dirty blonde hair. And with whom we had always had an easy time of it. He'd just sort of usher us through this thing then the next, the two days a week he was on. Then pack us off to bed. More a baby-sitter than a counselor.

Burl is strictly hands-on.

We're sitting in the TV room doing homework one evening when Mitch steps in the room.

"H-he wants Bobby," he says. His voice shaking. "Upstairs. Now."

Bobby gets up from the table. Eyebrows wondering. And goes up the stairs. A few seconds later, we hear *Whack. Whack. Whack.* Loud enough to make it down the stairs. And Bobby comes back down in tears. Rubbing his behind. The first in a whole line of guys to have the same fate befall them as the weeks of Mr. Gomillion's dominion over us stalk by, one by one. He never raises his voice with us. But doesn't have to, really. Behind every lift of his eyebrow, every sudden silence, lurks the threat of his huge right hand. And you never know until it is too late that you have transgressed an article of his unspoken code. You only find out after dinner. When he calls your name. And you make that terrified death march up to the second floor. It's tiptoes and whispers Mondays and Tuesdays when he is here. We're all scared to death of him.

Louie is soon replaced too. A guy named Samara. From Harlem. And black as a lump of coal, as my mother would say. A scrawny kid. Whose African ancestry seems etched on his every plane. A thing that leads us all to assume his name is African, too. Which it isn't. He comes from a huge family. A fact that isn't long in getting around. Thirteen brothers and sisters. All of whom have odd, alien-sounding names. Like "Will-ah-mean-ah" and "Jar-head." It becomes the big joke about him. To yell *Roll call!* Then rattle off the roster of his siblings in rapid succession. A thing that seldom fails to wound and confound him.

I never join in on picking on him. Nor does Pee Wee. To my surprise. But neither do he nor I find our way to befriending him. Me, because I am too embarrassed for him. Like when I catch him in the shower his first morning here. Sniffing at a bar of soap. Inhaling the sweetness of its fragrance before he uses the thing. More than being embarrassed for him, I'm embarrassed *by* him. That he never had it so good. And could care less who knows it.

He all but races to the dining hall at mealtime. Is always the first to ask for seconds. Even thirds. And his delight is obvious when the answer is yes. We watch him blossom out before our eyes. Within a month he's put on what must be fifty pounds. All but bursting out of his school-issue clothes. Which he tore into with breathless, Christmas-morning gusto, the day he got them. Then strutted around like a king wearing them. Living *high on the hog*, as my mother would say. It's all too close for comfort for me. I shrink from knowing him.

One day Steve has an announcement for me. He's no longer to be called by the same last name. "My mother got married again. I-I have a new father now," he tells me. I don't much like the new last name. It has too many syllables. I stick to calling him Steve. Two weeks later there's another surprise. I find him sitting on his bed when I come up to put away my books. Staring at the floor. I ask him if anything's wrong and he tells me no. That it's good news, actually.

"I'm outta' here," he grins. "I'm going home!"

I tell him "Great!" And pat him on the back. But as his remaining days wind down practically everything he does gets on my nerves. I snap at him. Take pot shots at his voice and ears. I hate that I do this. It is small and petty and I know it. But I can't stop myself. None of it really does the job either. There is never even a hint that I have wounded him. Even down to his last day here. When he comes up the stairs to get the last of his bags. To haul out to his new dad's shiny new car. When he halts, for the last time, by the door, and puts out his hand, I cannot dredge up the proper spirit. Just a "Well" and a "So!" And a scrunched-in, hands-in-my-pocket shrug. There is a hug. Chest and shoulders crowding in. I cling a bit too long.

"I'll writecha," he squeaks.

"Okay," I say. Halfway between grasping to this hope and knowing he never will. A week or so later another new kid is moved in. A big-headed, platinum-haired boy. Right away I decide I have no use for him. As the days bend toward Christmas loneliness descends. They don't do Christmas here. They do Chanukah. Except for the surrounding evergreens, there's no sign of it at all. No *Merry Christmas* banners in our classrooms. No glittering tree at the house. No one singing "Deck the Halls." And the hard rule of Mr. Gomillion two days a week to boot.

I'm down in the living room doing my homework one night after dinner. Starting with vocabulary. Leaving math for last. I hate math. There's nothing of yourself you can put into the mix. It has no poetry to it. It's one of Mr. Gomillion's absolute rules. That all homework must be done before the TV goes on. And I finish the vocabulary stuff. And am halfway through equations. When ping-pong Steve comes to get me. And the look on his face tells me all I need to know.

"He wants to see you," he says. "Upstairs."

An inventory of every big or small thing I could have done wrong goes through my head. As I close my math book and rise from the chair. Then trembling trepidation. When she used to spank me, my mother would punctuate each blow with a word. And at this she was always painfully verbose, as in *DON'T. YOU. EVER. LET. ME. CATCH. YOU. DOING. THAT. KIND. OF. FOOLISHNESS. EVER. AGAIN. DO. YOU. HEAR. ME!*

She hasn't spanked me in years, though. The people at the guidance center had advised her that I was full of rage. That hitting me would do no good. She took this to heart and never spanked me again. Went out and bought me a big, inflatable roly-poly clown. To take my anger out on. It was made of vinyl. And had a roundish base filled with sand. When you whacked him one he laid down, then stood right back up. And put that insipid smile of his in your face again. I didn't have the thing two weeks before I whopped it so hard it exploded.

When I get upstairs I see Pee Wee standing there. Then Samara. We eyeball each other. As Mr. Gomillion, arms across his chest, eyeballs us.

"Get your coats," he tells us.

We go off in different directions. Then assemble before him again in the hall. A few minutes later another counselor arrives and calls up the stairs. Mr. Gomillion leans over the banister. Says "Okay, Gill." And tells us, "C'mon." We go outside, into the crisp December air. To his car. An old green thing. With boxes and cans and blankets scattered about the back seat. Stand around looking at the thing.

"What are you waiting for," Mr. Gomillion says. "Get in."

The three of us make space amidst the back-seat clutter. We roll off the grounds. Where it is definitely Christmas. Bright decorations. Blinking lights. Plastic Santas and baby Jesuses everywhere. The three of us are silent. None of us daring to utter a word. As

Mr. Gomillion pilots the car onto the parkway. And we furrow into the black of the night. The edge of it held back by the lamps' halos overhead. It's warm and snug in the car. I can hear the tires hum as we buzz along.

After a while we turn off onto an exit ramp. The streets narrow into a little town. The houses are not quite as grand as some of those we have passed so far. But there are lights in the windows. And smoke curls from a chimney or two. We pull into a stingy driveway. Next to a narrow, brown and gray speckled, clapboard house. Mr. Gomillion gets out of the car. Which springs up a slight notch when relieved of his heft. We hustle to follow him. Up to the porch. He knocks on the door. A light jumps to life above his head. The door yawns open. A big dark woman. In a dime-store wig. Peers out. A smile breaks out on her face when she sees who it is. Screams of surprise and delight. She throws her huge arms around Mr. Gomillion. Peers at us over his shoulder.

"Who is this you have with you?" she says.

"Some of my kids," Mr. Gomillion says.

She corrals us all through the door.

Inside there is too much heat. And too much furniture. In one corner of the room sits a tree. With too many decorations. There are also too many people for the size of the room. Brothers. Sisters. Aunts. Uncles. Cousins. Friends. Too many for me to remember names when they are introduced. Or who each is to whom. There are cookies and cakes and cider and soda, and little gifts for each of us. I blush at each thing as it comes my way.

After a half hour or so we hit the road again. I'm homesick as soon as the car pulls away. But it is only a matter of minutes. Before we pull up to another narrow house. And do the same routine all over again. And, after that, yet another one. Mr. Gomillion saying nothing through all of it. Just silently herding us to one happy, Christmassy, house full of colored folk after another.

A giddy and breathless spree for me. I love the night. Have always loved it. It has always called to me. Lying in bed in Mamaroneck, listening through the still, suburban stillness, it was never the cicada's rasp but the growl and groan of distant traffic along the thruway that wooed me. Tossed and turned me. Filled me with a dark and sad ache, a cold loneliness. That was never once not utterly seductive. And I would pine to be out there in that inky void. Where the highway lights were strung like jewels. I don't know why.

It is near midnight when we finally head back for the campus. Pee Wee so bowled over he doesn't speak. Samara with a schoolboy grin so wide he's nothing but teeth. Mr. Gomillion in stony contentment. He flips on the radio and it is R&B all the way home. Marvin Gaye. The Supremes. Ben E. King singing,

There is a rose in Span-ish Har-lem

A red rose up in Span-ish Har-lem.

I have never been to Harlem. And thinking *Harlem-Samara*, I look at him. His eyes shut. His head swaying back and forth. I close my eyes, too. Put a picture of Harlem in my mind. As I imagine it must be at night. Streetlights spilling onto the pavement. Smashing against the rude, goblin green of fluorescents, glaring from storefront windows. Cars swinging around corners. The sudden swell and falter of headlights bleaching everything they touch to blue-white brilliance. And everywhere people out. Dark faces silhouetted. Lights winking, blinking, shimmering, screaming. Railing against the darkness.

I see myself. There amid the throngs. Longings I never knew I had bubbling up in me. As I stroll along. Off to nowhere in particular. Gathering answers to questions I have not yet found the words to ask.

When I open my eyes again I see we are cruising toward Linda Avenue. Which winds itself right up to the campus gate. It feels like we have been away for a week. The DJ on the radio says he has a "Golden

Oldie" for us next. Lloyd Price. Singing *Personality*. Mr. Gomillion lets out a loud *Hah!, t*he only sound he has made the whole trip. And cranks the volume up. When the chorus comes on we all chime in. Our clashing voices falling in together on the last line, *Cause you got a great big hear-ar-ar-t!* We sing right through the gate, up the hill, to the cottage door.

28

On the inside of my left forearm I have a pair of scars. One, just over an inch long, right beneath the palm. And another longer scar about four inches further down. I got them when I was nine. Just before Christmas. My mother was off doing day work to earn some extra cash. So Wayne and I were home alone. I was chasing him for some reason. I can't remember what it was. Playing, though. It wasn't a fight or anything like that. Just horsing around. And he ran into our room. Which has a french door. The kind that is mostly little glass windows. I was running so hard when he slammed the door I couldn't stop in time. My arm went right through one of the panes. And got torn open on the glass. Then I tore it open again yanking my arm back out.

There was lots of blood. It came out in spurts. One for each throb of my pulse. And I went a little nuts when I saw it. Ran into the hallway screaming. Wanting it to be a dream but knowing it wasn't. Scaring everyone in the house half to death. The first one to get to me was Tootsie. She came racing down the stairs. Her hair all up in curlers.

"Oh my God, Caverly," she said. When she saw all the blood spurting out. "Somebody call an ambulance!"

That frightened me more than my wound. The way I feel about ambulances. Which is that I could just as well do without ever seeing another one. With my mother it's hospitals. The year before, I got a fishhook caught in my thumb. Fooling around with a fishing rod I had found in the dump behind the lot across the street. My mother and Wayne weren't home. A Sunday morning. I had wormed my way out of going to church.

The fishing line got tangled when I tried to cast it, and swung back. Buried the hook in my thumb. And I couldn't pull it out. Not with the barb and all. So I put a Band-Aid just beneath where the hook was sticking out and went to bed. I couldn't think of what else to do. When my mother got home and I showed her the thing she just collapsed into a chair and started crying. My mother really bawls when she cries. Almost like a kid. She has the saddest cry I've ever heard. Alma, from upstairs, had to take me to the emergency room. My mother just couldn't bring herself to do it.

But it's ambulances with me. And when Tootsie mentioned calling one I sort of went into a panic. Started running up and down the hall screaming *"No! No! No!"* Like someone was trying to kill me or something. Tootsie had to slap me one to bring me back to my senses. It took thirteen stitches to patch me up. I came back home with my left arm in a sling. My mother was home by then. Looking worse for wear than me.

"Thank God I wasn't here to see it," she said.

She put me to bed early. Came in the room with a brown bag. Plopped it down on the bed.

"I was going to give you these for Christmas," she said. "But in view of what happened you can have them now."

The bag was full of comics. Marvel comics. *Spiderman. The Hulk. The Fantastic Four.* Which are a little cheaper than DC comics. The home of Superman, Batman, and so forth. Only I ended up liking these much better. The drawings in DC comics are mostly line and color. But these had light and shadow too. Used to great dramatic effect. Like a movie. And sometimes the action scenes would spill across two or three panels. Like it was jumping right off the page.

My favorite of them all was Spiderman. Who wears glasses. The same as me. And who has all this stuff happening inside, just like me. Which no one else seems to ever understand. A superhero just for me. Who always beats the bad guy. He's pretty good at that. But when it comes to getting along in the world, has a harder time of it. Same as me.

There were three *Spidermans* in the bunch. I read them all three in a row. Forgot all about the ambulance. And my throbbing arm. Just ate them up. One after another. And when I finished the last panel in the last one, I set it down and cried a little. A happy kind of cry, because all the while I was reading them it was like having a little voice in my head telling me *you are not alone.*

I'm thinking about all this because they've moved me. Usually, fourteen years old is the age for switching to the intermediate unit. But I've sprouted up pretty good over the last year. And I guess this has led whoever makes such decisions to suppose I'd be better off amongst bigger kids. Even though I'm still thirteen. So here I am now. A couple hundred paces up campus. In Cottage Fifteen. And one of the first things I discover is that Arty, one of my new roommates, has comics. In spades. At least a hundred of them stashed under his bed. Which is catty-corner next to mine. And every time his father visits, he brings up a fresh armful of them. From the candy store he owns, Arty tells me.

Arty's the kind of guy you'd expect in a place like this. He's got the hood thing going. Wears black Levis all the time. With ankle-high boots. Keeps the sleeves of his t-shirt rolled back. And walks with a little hitch in his stride. Which makes the arc of his pompadour bob with every step.

He spits a lot, too. Seems to have a whole repertoire of them in fact. Three that I've counted so far. The *blow spit.* Where his cheeks puff up and the snotty gob is launched aloft with a flick of his tongue. The juicier *zip spit.* Which, since it is fired off through the teeth, he is able to aim with remarkable accuracy. And the basic *pachew! spit.* Expelled casually but explosively. With a quick turn of the head. Like casting off a sudden bad taste.

He's got a pretty good temper, too. Only not like the rest of us. Who go hot when we get our hairs up. Arty goes cold. Ice cold. Cross a line with him and he's relentless. It's all or nothing. Scorched-earth time. I know this because I'm not here two days before I get a taste of it. We're up in the room talking comics. Me going on about Spiderman. And Arty going on about Batman. And somewhere in there he says Spiderman's a wimp. Because he stays with his aunt. And his life is a mess. And the other guys at school push him around. And, exasperated that he completely misses the point, I tell him, "You're crazy."

He looks at me. A hard and dangerous look. Blinks. Then blinks again. His eyes seeming to go from brown to black. Something bottomless and implacable as stone seeping into them. As if it were all a foregone conclusion what would happen next. And all that's left to do is settle on where to bury my remains.

His shoulders stiffen. And his arm falls to his side. And kind of swings behind him. When it swings forward again, there's a knife in his hand. Not just any knife either. Not the kind of knife you use for cutting rope. Or gutting fish. Or to slice your steak into bite-size pieces. A switchblade knife. The kind of knife you only use for one reason. For stabbing people.

Then I see his thumb move down the handle. See it press the little button in the middle. See the blade swing out. Hear the *click* of it snapping into place. And flinch. My eyes bringing the lids down all by themselves. A universe of blackness closing in for a fraction of a second. And then squinting when they pop back open again. To see if I see what I think I'm seeing. That it isn't really a blade at all. But a . . . comb. Made up to look like one. A switchblade comb.

"Neat," I tell the off-angle grin on Arty's face. Thinking it isn't neat at all. Then his eyes go off of me. And he uses the thing. Gives his hair a half-dozen slow, practiced strokes. Raking the gleaming black strands back into arching, striated rows. Which terminate in a ducktail at the nape of his neck. Then he gingerly pinches out a gaggle of eagle's claws in front. And tickles them into a pompadour.

Such a cool move.

A thing I will never be able to do.

He studies me again for a few seconds. As he stows the phony dagger back on his hip. His face collecting itself, then softening out again. As if he'd made up his mind about something.

"So," he says, "you smoke?"

I mumble that of course I do.

And the air that has fled the room comes back again.

We go outside. Arty scraping together a viscous nugget of throat debris, soon as we're out in the sun. Which he *thwacks* to the sidewalk with the utmost disdain. I follow him to the tool shed out back. To the cover of its far side. He pulls a pack of Marlboros out of his boot when we get there and fires one of them up. He doesn't offer me one. So I stand there watching him smoke. Increasingly absorbed in how he handles a cigarette. He doesn't take puffs. He *yank*s drags from the thing. Snatches it from his mouth. Lets the smoke curl up over his lip. And pulls it in through his nose. A "French inhale," he tells me. Another cool move.

"So. Your pop owns a candy store," I say. Fishing to ease things off the rest of the way. And maybe get in on a drag or two to boot.

"Yeah," he says. But without conviction.

"Must be pretty neat," I say.

"Yeah," he says again and pops off a trio of large, lazy smoke rings. Sends a missile of phlegm arcing behind them. Then hands the cigarette to me. And walks off. It's almost down to the filter. Maybe two drags left. Two tries at doing the French inhale and blowing smoke rings.

29

We're down in the basement rec room. And Mitch, one of my new cottage mates, pulls his head out of the refrigerator. "Okay," he says. His brows narrowed into a *V.* Peering around the room. Taking inventory of who is gnawing on what. "Who's the sonova bitch who took my Reese's?" Mitch is usually a pretty benign guy. One of the many kids up here to make you wonder whatever it was they possibly could have done to get themselves sent to this place. I can't say I've ever seen him get in anyone's face.

But it happens to be snack time. And snack time happens to be a volatile thing. Because there are not just house snacks to contend with. There are *private snacks* too. Something we didn't have at Cottage Five. You got whatever was served. Everybody the same. Here, there's a refrigerator for us. And it's forever stuffed with the extra eats everybody loads up on when their parents visit. Pies. Cookies. Cakes. Sodas. Juices. Fruit rolls. Crackers. Cheeses. Chips. Dips. Cold cuts. Chicken. Pastries. And candy, of course. Of every size and substance. You'd think they aren't feeding us here, to see it all.

Part of it seems to be a keeping up with the Joneses kind of thing. One guy seeing what the next guy's got and trying to outdo him. Like putting a pool in your back yard because the people next door have one. When snack time rolls around it's all elbows and arms and rubbing shoulders at the refrigerator door. Followed by an orgy of conspicuous consumption. In which the haves lord it over the have-nots. With precious little sharing across the line. The well-lardered tending to go with the well-lardered as surely as money goes with money.

I have tried to enlist my mother into the spirit of this private snacks thing. But she doesn't seem to get it. She remains ever modest and practical in what she brings. A small box of miniature chocolate chip cookies, one visit. A single bag of nickel chips the next. Always something I can consume in one sitting. The idea that I must have enough to sustain me over the week ahead eludes her. So whereas I would otherwise be grateful for any extra thing she might bring, I am instead embarrassed that it is not more than it is.

On the other hand this leaves me with nothing to protect. And therefore out of the kind of fray that Mitch is angling towards as his eyes land on Arty. Who's reading a *Green Hornet* comic. Chewing a candy bar. Sitting all the way across the room. Which is him all the way. I've never seen him go near anything that has even a whiff of being a group activity. He keeps a scornful distance from the rest of us. And expects the same in return. Violate the space he's staked out for himself and you're in for more hassle than it's worth.

I still have no idea what it was that stopped him from taking things all the way with me. For calling him crazy. But the next time I saw him all was forgotten. He was on his way down to the pines. And asked me to come along. He had a homemade slingshot with him and a pocketful of marbles. "To kill a few squirrels," he told me. I wasn't all too hot on doing this. But I scrambled to catch up to him anyway.

We didn't kill anything, as it turned out. But not for lack of trying. Just that we couldn't find any squirrels about. Arty tried for a jay. Or whatever it was. Chirping and flapping up in the branches. But the thing just flew away. So it was a cigarette instead. And oysters of Arty's phlegm smacking against the trunks of the trees. And finally he gave it up.

"We can come back again tomorrow," he said.

I took particular note of the "we."

For some reason Arty seems to have settled on me. Has adopted me, pretty much, as a worthy partner in crime. Someone with whom to break the rules. A thing that seems to heighten everything. And from which I find myself getting immense satisfaction. Like Arty's comics. It's so much more exciting reading them by flashlight. The two of us hunched under a blanket on his bed. Even though he always trains the center of the beam his way when it's his turn to hold the light. Leaving the dim edge to me. Having a cigarette, too. All the richer tasting when smoked on the sly at night. Even though I have yet to get a whole one from Arty. Only his dregs.

Arty pretty much thinks of himself first in most things, when you get right down to it. I'm just along for the ride. A hitchhiker on whatever mischievous whim he might entertain. I find I don't mind this all that much. His selfishness. I even find a kind of comfort in it. That it's blessedly free of stakes. That there's nothing at risk of being betrayed. It's enough for me just knowing that whatever war Arty's got going with the world, it doesn't seem to include the likes of me.

Mitch, though, isn't so lucky. Two healthy chews into his Reese's Peanut Butter Cup, Arty notices Mitch looking at him. And blinks. Twice. Each flutter of his lids working like windshield wipers. Polishing the surface of his eyes to gleaming, black stone.

You might figure that, with his father owning a whole candy store, Arty wouldn't have any reason to steal the stuff. Only candy's the one thing I've never seen his parents bring him. Just comics, mostly. And none of those are new. The title and date are always torn from their covers.

Mitch doesn't say anything. He isn't stupid. He knows he is teetering on the edge of an abyss. That once you get Arty going there's no turning him off. He pulls his eyes away. And slinks to a chair on the opposite side of the room. Like a boxer going to his corner of the ring. Only when he sits, he makes just a hint of a show of it. Twists his face up in disgust and bangs his butt down.

Arty lowers his comic now.

That same dead look in his eyes he'd put on me.

"You got some kind of problem?" he says.

And there is no mistaking it as a question. Or anything other than the dare it is. Mitch, a cauldron of suppressed fire now. Even as Arty goes cooler by the second. Knowing just where he's going to take this thing.

"I didn't say anything," Mitch says. And it is almost enough. Except that he adds, "Okay?" An altogether slender bit of defiance. But plenty enough for Arty.

"Yeah you did," Arty says. The comic now in his lap. The Reese's which started the whole thing long since gone. "You're trying to make like it was me who took your shit."

"No—"

"Oh, so now I'm a liar," Arty says. "First you call me a thief. Now you're saying I'm a liar."

Everyone goes quiet. It's damned if you do, damned if you don't for Mitch now. Arty's always been very public in promising to knock the teeth clean out of anyone calling him a liar. No one moves a muscle. Except for me. Angling around a little bit for a better view. And in the sudden stillness I hear a familiar plod. Beyond the rec room wall. Mr. Gruzman. The house father. Clunking down the stairs. The muted click of his heels on the concrete floor as he comes around through the door. All eyes go to the door.

"Vat is happen here?" he says. And our eyes leave him. We are all suddenly fascinated with the floor. He steps to the center of the room. Smoldering cigarette scissored between his fingers. Draws back his suit jacket and parks his fist on his hip.

"I ask a question. Vat is happen here."

No one answers him.

When I first met him and his wife I only had eyes for what was different about them. Having never met any real Russians before. All I'd ever heard about that part of the world was that it's filled with tyranny, misery and black intrigues. That there's not enough to go around. And endless lines for everything.

I took in Zunya's square, Frankenstein head. His pallid skin. The darkness around his hard, gray eyes. Notice his sharp, beveled jaw was blue with five o'clock shadow. Even though it was just after breakfast. I saw the tips of his first two fingers are browned and slightly dented, when we shook hands. He smokes short, unfiltered cigarettes. Went through two of them in the few minutes that we talked. Puffing on them with a fury. Two or three pulls just to stoke the thing up before he inhaled. Smoked them both down until the flame was at his knuckles. Then ground the stub to smithereens in the ashtray.

He tried for a smile when he shook my hand. But his face does not wear it well. He has no lips. Just a slash where his mouth should be.

"Ca-va-lee." he repeated. Thoughtfully. When I pronounced my name for him. "Where did you get zis name?"

Mrs. Gruzman was easier to take. Her smile lit up her weary face. She took my hand in hers when we shook. Covered it with the other. Said, "How do you do Cav-ver-lee." Hitting each syllable evenly. Her eyes fluttered and swooned when she spoke. A disarming thing. She struck me as kind of a gypsy. What I imagine one to be at least. Jet-black hair. Long eyelashes. And the kind of spirit that would rather dance the night away, say, than indulge in bitterness.

"Please," she said. When I called her Mrs. Gruzman. "You vill call me Mom, no?"

I blushed a little at that. Then looked back at Mr. Gruzman. Tried to imagine the same thing for him. Me calling him "Pop." I still can't seem to make it fit though.

"Okay." he says. Tapping his foot on the concrete floor. "Ziz is fine. You do not want to make an answer. Good. Up za stairs now!" Clapping his hands together. "Everyone. Snack time is over."

We file up to the TV room. Arty with his jaw still up, I see. And Mitch hovering by Mr. Gruzman. I feel cheated. I was really hoping to see the whole thing come to a head. To see for myself what Arty's got in there. What kind of riot would come galloping out of him and stampede upon Mitch's curly little head. I have nothing against Mitch. I even feel sorry for him. Getting himself all jammed up like that. But this is snack time at Cottage Fifteen. I'm merely a peasant spectator. The show of it is all I've got.

Mitch manages to cut a wide enough berth around Arty for the next few days that, despite the steam Arty holds at the ready for him, it never gets the chance to blow. However much nothing is either forgiven or forgotten. And not to be totally daunted, Mitch comes up with a bright idea. He gets a magic marker and initials everything in the refrigerator that belongs to him. It quickly catches on. And once it does, there's no knowing you own a thing but that it bears your brand. So things go up another notch, as anything not marked comes to be taken for fair game. And it becomes a new necessity of snack time that we take refuge in the rites of ownership. None of us taking the slightest notice, as we blunder into this new business, that its first casualty is that nothing anymore can be left to trust.

30

The flu is going around. And it's got our regular English teacher out sick. Mr. Horowitz is substituting. And has had us reading short stories. One a day. Out loud. And in turn. Then he wants to know what we think the story's about. Not just what happens, but what it's about. A thing he calls subtext. A word I like right away.

Yesterday it was a pretty neat story about a big lottery drawing in a little town. Everyone gets a ticket. And they're all hepped up about it. It's the only thing they talk about. Only in the end instead of the person with the winning number getting a prize, everyone gathers up rocks and stones her to death. I'm still a little fuzzy on what the subtext of that one was.

Today's story is little closer to home for me. About a stranger who moves into a small town. Where everybody knows everybody else. And he quickly becomes the talk of the town. There's something "different" about him, everyone keeps saying. Mostly because he keeps to himself. Doesn't try to mix in with anyone else. He's not an unpleasant fellow. Doesn't have any bad habits. Doesn't do anything wrong. Just keeps to himself. And that drives the whole town kind of crazy. They go from being suspicious of him to being afraid of him, to wanting to ride him out of town on a rail.

Right off I thought of Arty. Loner that he is. And I got the small town thing, too. Everyone knowing everyone else. And leery of any new face that shows itself. It stirred up how small and ugly and kind of dirty not fitting in always leaves me feeling. Only in the story you get the sense that it's the other way around. It's the townspeople. The ones who put you down for being different. Who are small and ugly and dirty.

"So," Mr. Horowitz says when we get to the end. "What do we make of this. What do you think Tennessee Williams might have been trying to say in telling this tale?"

I throw a hand up.

"You can't judge a book by its cover?"

One of my mother's sayings. It seemed to fit.

"Ye-e-es," Mr. Horowitz says. "Good, CAVE-early. Very good." He beams at me as he says it, too. A gratifying thing. Putting the sunshine in a teacher's face like that.

"They have a word for this," he says. "For when you pre-judge someone. Anyone know what that word is?"

I raise my hand again. Tell him, "prejudice." And again he beams at me.

"Exactly," he says. "Can anyone give me an example of this?"

A fat kid named Kevin. Who always breathes through his mouth. Tells the class about being down South one summer with his family. And saw how awfully they treated "their colored people."

"I wouldn't want to be a Negro down South," he says.

Then it's Mike Seigel. Who's in Cottage Fifteen with me. Letting us know that he's from the South originally. And that they don't have any great love for Jews down there either. I hadn't considered this before. That there was all that much difference between the lot of one set of lucky sons and the next. I just figured that, like Kevin said, they were all well enough off not to have been born Negro.

We go around with this stuff for the rest of the period. About Martin Luther King. And the Ku Klux Klan. And integration and so forth. Not my favorite subjects. Not when I'm the only one in the room, if you know what I mean. We talk about ignorance and fear, too. Mr. Horowitz does, anyway. Once you have fear, he tells us, it's a very short trip to anger and rage.

Then he comes out with something that makes the thing I don't want to happen happen. He supposes that, in the scheme of things, perhaps

Negroes were put here on this earth for the purpose of teaching man tolerance. Half the class turns to gape at me when he says it. That thing all over again. And I hear a snort. From Mike Seigel. Who sits across from me. Then he blows a raspberry at me. Looks over. Curls up his lip. And lets off a real pig snort of a blast. Even Mr. Horowitz hears it. And gives him one of those *I'm-going-to-stand-here-and-stare-at-you-until-you-get-the-message* kind of looks. Seigel loses the sneer. But his nose stays wrinkled up. Like someone just cut a humdinger of a fart. A look I know is meant for me.

I burnt my bridges with him a long time ago. Even before I switched cottages. I upped and belted him one. Out of the blue. And for no other reason but to see if it were really possible. To knock a guy out with a single punch. I got the idea from watching TV. A Western that comes on every week called *The Rebel.* One of my favorite shows. It's a little like the Tennessee Williams story in a way. About a guy who doesn't fit in. And doesn't do things the way everyone else does. Only this guy was once a soldier. And got booted from the army for it. So now he just kind of roams from town to town. Trying to outrun the disgrace of his dishonorable discharge, I guess. And every week he ends up doing something more honorable than everybody else and ending up a hero.

Of course you can't be a real hero without being ready to fight. At least not on TV, anyway. And one night, after seeing him put a guy's lights out with one blow, I got the idea that if I could do this myself, if I knew it would just be the one punch, I might be able to stand my ground if any of the guys ever call me out.

So I was just itching for a chance, when I saw Mike standing there. A kind of a pretty-boy, if you want to know the truth. And a little on the stuck-up side, too. Not hoity-toity stuck up, exactly. Just that he has a way, when he wants to, of treating you like you don't exist. Like it would kill him to say boo to you.

I hauled off and gave him one to the jaw. Only I was off a hair. And felt the peculiar sensation of my fist bashing into something hard and sharp. Those pearly white teeth of his. I didn't knock him out either. He didn't even go down. What I did manage to do was piss him off. He hit me with a right cross. It came out of nowhere. Slammed into the side of my head so hard I saw stars and ended up in the infirmary. With a perforated eardrum and a swollen fist. Not to mention half a week's worth of pain and a week on dep. A real fiasco all around.

So there's no way anyone's going to convince Seigel that this Negro has the slightest thing to teach him about tolerance. To tell the truth I'm not all that thrilled Mr. Horowitz brought the whole thing up. Even though I think he said it for my benefit. Sometimes I wish that there were no races. That we were all blended together. And there were no lines between this guy and the next. So that even I could be happy. Like everybody else.

"Wait!" Mr. Horowitz says when the bell finally rings. And we all scramble. It being Friday. "Homework," he tells us. "I want 300 words on tolerance from each of you. Monday."

The good thing about Friday assignments is that you have the weekend. And I have no intention of getting down to it until the last minute. But I'm thinking about it while we're walking back to the house. Daydreaming, kind of. About a world where there's no black or white. And everyone getting along. Thinking maybe I'll write something about that. And somewhere in there the phrase "all blended to-ge-ther," and the phrase "would be so much bet-ter" fall one after the other. And as I'm going upstairs to put my school things away, another two lines pop into my head. "A better place resulting in just one race." So instead of stowing my books, I pull out my notebook and start scratching away.

Next thing you know, it's heading towards five o'clock. Everyone getting ready for the Friday thing. And I remember my wrinkled slacks. And have to stop. To go downstairs. And see if I can get a turn at the house iron. Another thing we didn't have at Cottage Five. It's an old, clunky thing, though. Barely a match for my stiff old pair of school-issue Farah slacks. And I'm leaning on the thing so hard the ironing board creaks and sags under my weight. Trying to get a crease to hold. When Mr. Gruzman comes up behind me.

"No, no. Not like zis," he says. "Wait I show you."

He disappears into his apartment. Comes back out carrying a glass of water and a newspaper.

"Here, put za paper," he tells me, handing it to me. Pointing to my slacks.

I do this. Spread the paper over the slacks. Even though I feel a little silly doing it. He hands me the glass of water. Pantomimes that I should take a gulp. Which makes even less sense. I do it anyway. Wolfing down a huge mouthful.

"No," Zunya says. Exasperated. "Not to swallow!" He billows up his sallow cheeks. To show I should keep the water in my mouth.

"Take again," he says.

I get a good mouthful and turn to him. With an okay, what's next look on my face.

"Now," he says, pursing his lips, "Blow!"

I just stare at him for a few seconds.

"On za paper," he says, "Blow. Is good. You see."

By now I have an audience. A couple of guys. One of them grinning at me. The other frowning. I do as Mr. Gruzman says. Spray blotches of water all over the newspaper. And get a few giggles for my trouble.

"Now." Mr. Gruzman says. Making ironing motions with his hand. "Go ahead. Continue."

I go to take the newspaper off.

"No!" he says. Sucking his teeth. "Like zis. Leave za paper."

I do this. Steam spitting out the sides of the iron. And it works like a charm. I am able to put a crease in my pants sharp enough to slice cheese. I look back at Mr. Gruzman. Who nods his head and grins. In perfect disharmony to the hard, gaunt lines of his face. And the sheer poetry of it. That two utterly humble items could be put to use in this way. Opens me up to Mr. Gruzman in an unexpected way. And for the first time I am able to wrap myself around the idea, at least, of thinking of him as Pop. Maybe not the Pop of my birth. Maybe not a Pop Bedford, even. But, for all his idiosyncrasies, a Pop nonetheless.

We muster outside. March to the dining hall. Me still concocting a rhyme in my head. We do the Friday ritual. Then we all eat fried chicken. Me watching Pop Gruzman. Who eats his with a knife and fork. And it strikes me. I almost laugh out loud. Here we all are. A white, black, Jewish, Russian, fried chicken-eating amalgamation. All sitting here together. As natural as can be. All blended together after all. All you have to do is look for it. And there it is! For the rest of the meal. And all the way back to the cottage. And even while I am at my homework. The same tune keeps playing in my head.

From the mountains . . .

To the prairies . . .

To the oceans . . .

White with foam . . .

But then comes snack time.

We all hustle for the rec room. Which looks a little like the Port Authority bus depot now. A riot of wooden lockboxes. Of all shapes and sizes. Every one with a lock dangling from it. I don't remember who was the first to build one of these things. But Mike Seigel took the cake at it. Came out of school one day barely able to carry the masterpiece he had constructed in shop. A veritable personal pantry. Made of pine and plywood. Stained and varnished to look like oak. With counter-sunk brass hinges. Beveled edges. Molding along the bottom. And on the lip of the lid, a big brass hinge and clasp. For the Master combination lock.

If anyone thought this kind of thing would solve the problem, though, they had it wrong. All it did was up the stakes. Not long after the private boxes began to appear, the unwritten rule went from anything not monogrammed being fair game, to anything not locked down.

And the onset of snack time soon became a more covert bustle, as the haves crowded in close to dial out their combinations, away from the prying eyes of the have-nots.

Despite all the industry, however, those who want in are not to be denied. A pried hinge. A few loosened screws. Is all it takes. So the injury of property took its place beside the insult of theft. And snack time has gradually devolved. By angry, suspicious, alienating degrees into what is an often-ugly clash. Accusations. Threats. Screaming fits. And out-and-out fist fights began to flare up between the petty, the larcenous, the miserly, the envious, the smug and the wanting.

One night things got so bad that Doc, the relief counselor, declared a moratorium on private snacks for the night. House snacks only. Peanut butter and jelly for everyone. But confrontation ruled nonetheless as we lined up to construct our sandwiches. Bickering broke out over the amount of jelly people were putting on their bread. Those at the tail of the queue fearing the jelly would run out before they got to it. Exasperated, Doc took over. Emptied both jars into a big bowl. And kneaded them together with his fingers. Until it was all one red-brown goo. This brought down a whole new wall. Doc's black hands having actually touched the food. Half the guys decided that they weren't all that hungry after all.

A spectacle now, snack time.

I've got all the show I could want.

When we get downstairs and everyone heads for their boxes, Mr. Gruzman stations himself in the middle of the room. Also a part of the routine now. Him standing there. Like a sheriff. To keep a lid on things. And always a bit disturbed and chagrined by this duty. After all, talk about subtext, he and Mrs. Gruzman had traveled I don't know how many thousands of miles for the hope of just this, the sanctity of personal possessions. He finds his moment though. With Barry's mother.

Barry's remarkable only in his utter plainness, his ghostly pallor, and his immense, untoned girth. He's constantly the brunt of jokes and pranks. Like the night a couple of the guys "share" half a dozen of their "chocolates" with him. During snacks. It isn't until a couple of hours or so later, when a sudden urgency sends Barry barreling for the toilet, that the chocolates are revealed to be doses of Ex-Lax.

We hear about it that Sunday. Loud and clear. From Barry's mother, a tough-talking Brooklyn matriarch who seldom comes to visit without making herself known. And Barry, her only son, is the jewel of her eye. She stands up in the middle of visiting time and scolds our wanton cruelty. "A bunch of vicious hooligans," she calls us. Who should be ashamed of ourselves.

Yet this is mild stuff. In comparison to the stink she raises a few weeks later. Over Barry's missing apricot rolls. A thing I had never seen before. Fruit pressed into sheets.

"Outrageous!" we suddenly hear her roar. "Stealing?! What on earth is wrong with you kids!" she cries, rising from her seat. "Even thieves don't steal from each other!"

This sticks with me. Leaves me to wonder if it is true.

". . . a buncha cheap stinkin' bums," she adds, scowling around the room. Before she plops herself back down. A stony silence falls over the room. I hear my mother say, "My goodness." Then the rising purr of the other parents, who take quite an exception to their little darlings being referred to in such a manner. *And who is running this place, anyway? How could they let this mad woman disrespect our children so?*

"Don't you think that's a little unfair? Blaming everyone?" one of them speaks up. A father. Gray at the temples. In spectacles. Wearing a blue suit.

"A-a-h," Barry's mother scowls. "I wouldn't give a plug nickel for the lot of them and a song."

Another parent chimes in, a mother this time.

"And I suppose your son's a regular angel," she says. "Why else would he be up here?"

As good a question as any. Why any of us are up here. It goes unanswered though. They go back and forth. The grownups. Each time it gets a little uglier. Quite a spectacle for me, seeing grownups at each other's throats. The hubbub draws Mr. Gruzman into the living room. He tries to get a bead on what all the to-do is about. But everyone talks right through him. He has to raise his voice himself.

"Look at zis! You are supposed to be adults!" he barks. "And you are behave like children! Vat is zis?"

It quells the rising storm. But not before the blue-suit guy makes it clear that he is not at all pleased with things. And that we can all be sure he will have a word with the director of the school about it. For the rest of visiting time, we all keep our eyes on the food.

Mr. Horowitz will hold my effort worthy of only a C-plus when I hand in my homework on Monday. It's not the three-hundred-word essay he had asked us to do, but a dozen lines of rhyme. Not because he doesn't like my "poem," he is quick to let me know. But because I have to learn to follow the rules. The poem is very good, he tells me.

"Yes. Yes," he says. "You must keep writing."

That night Pop Gruzman gives us the news. That from hereon there will be no more private snacks. Communal snacks only.

"No more wid za boxes," he says, his voice low, almost broken. "Is finish."

A few months later, the TV program we are all watching is interrupted for a special news report. An historical moment, the newscaster says. Nikita Khrushchev, the premier of Russia, has stepped down.

"Leave zis," Mr. Gruzman says. When one of the guys reaches to change the channel. "I want to see."

He sits there. Ashtray in front of him. Working up a fearsome cloud of smoke. As the newsman goes on to talk about a possible "coup." He's impatient with me when I ask him what a coup is. "He was force to resign," is all he says. Still puffing away. Eyes on the TV screen all the time.

"Gee, Pop," one of the guys says. Going for a laugh. "You must be all broken up."

Mr. Gruzman doesn't find it funny. Maybe half a snicker gets out. Before he cuts it short. "DON'T SAY ZIS!" he barks. With such vehemence, spittle flies from his non-lips. "HE WAS CRAZY, THIS KHRUSHCHEV! HE WAS MAD MAN! IS GOOD HE IS GONE!"

31

It's around midnight, and Arty and I are having a cigarette. Crouched at the window in the locker alcove attached to our room. Blowing the smoke out into the night. Which belongs to us. There being no one around to say any different. David and Sudak are gone. Our other two roommates. Whom we more or less ignore anyway. Mom and Pop Gruzman are not down in their apartment. Emmett, the relief counselor who lives upstairs, is not here. The house is entirely absent of grownups. The whole campus is.

Then, a noise. Out on the landing.

The cigarette goes out the window and we make for our beds. But we are not entirely quick enough. The light snaps on. And there is a guy standing by the door. A James Dean-looking guy in blue jeans. Holding a flashlight. And wearing a telltale, gray, night watchman's shirt. His eyes zip, brisk and efficient, from point to point around the room. For a second it is so quiet, all you can hear is the hissing radiator.

"'Choo guys up to?" he says.

"Nothing," Arty tells him. "Just got up to open a window," he tells him. "It's too hot. I can't sleep."

The man tilts his head farther and farther back as he takes this in. So that he's now looking down the length of his nose at us.

"A window in the locker room," he says.

Arty blinks. I've never noticed it before. But his lashes are long and willowy.

"Yeah," he says. His weight going from right foot to left. "You don't want a draft right on ya'." Managing to put on an impatient, *I-shouldn't-*

have-to-be-telling-you-this tone. "Ya' catch ammonia havin' a draft right on ya'."

The night watchman nods slowly and his eyes go off us for a minute. Click off another half-dozen snapshots. Then settle on me.

"And it took both of you to do this?" he says.

"It sticks," I tell him. "You need two people to get it open."

Again the nod. And something just short of a half-smile. He puts his tongue inside of his cheek. Shakes his head. A couple of times up and down. Slowly. Then takes a few lazy strides toward the locker alcove. Until he's half a step in. And stops there. Looks around, but doesn't try the window. I take in an overdue breath.

"Can't sleep, huh?" he says. A little light in his eyes now. A cat that ate the canary kind of look. Then another search of our faces. And a few more blinks around the room.

"Well, come on."

We follow him into the hall. Then down the stairs. To a thermos sitting on the night table in the foyer. Which he grabs as we pass. We follow him into the living room. "Go ahead," he says, and sets down the thermos with a kind of sigh. "Grab yourselves a sit-down."

We plop down side by side on the couch. He turns on the TV.

Unscrews the cap of the thermos and half fills it with coffee. "Guys are lucky," he says and consults his watch. "As of three minutes ago I'm on my break." He passes the thermos lid to me. Nods from me to Arty. "I only got the one," he says. "You two'll have to share." I look at Arty. Arty looks at me. "Name's Luke, by the way," he says. "I'm part-time temporary. Sunday to Thursday. Till this thing's over. You guys bearing up okay?"

I tell him fine.

It was quite a shock at first. Three days ago now. Coming through the classroom doors after school and finding no one there but the principal. It was the first I ever heard about the union. The child-care workers union, he told us. To which just about all the adults here belong.

Including our house parents. A strange thing to imagine. A union of Moms and Pops. Strange even to think of them as workers. When it has always seemed they were simply part of our lives. Much less that they would go out on strike. A "job action," the principal called it. But it felt more like a betrayal to me.

Then next day they shipped off as many of us as they could. Sudak and David among them. To Children's Village. To Pleasantville Cottage School. And other nearby places like this. And brought in temporaries to fill in as house parents. A pair of Joe College types for us. Right down to their chinos, loafers and pastel-plaid print shirts. Easy-going guys. Whose primary concern, it seems, is that we like and accept them. They're always encouraging us to call them by their first names. And forever casting about for fun things we can do.

Plus, they go home at night. About a half-hour after we are put to bed. Except for the night watchman, who comes every hour to make his rounds, there's nobody here. You'd think this would add up to riot and chaos after lights out. Funny thing is, most of the guys cling to the usual routine. In lieu of other instruction, it's the only way they know to fill their days. Arty and I seem to be the only ones interested in making it up as we go along.

"Cheers," our new friend Luke says. He's found a Styrofoam cup somewhere. We toast with our coffees. It's on the sweet side. The way I like it. "You got about fifteen minutes, boys, then it's back to bed." He wiggles the fingers of his free hand into his breast pocket. Comes out with a pack of Luckies. Shakes it until a few sticks are peeking out of the top. Lips one of them into his mouth. All with one hand. Cool.

"Smoke?" he says.

I eye the pack suspiciously. Thinking, *got to be some kind of trap.* Arty says "No thanks." Then adds, on second thought, that they don't allow us to smoke. To which Luke kind of smiles. With the corner of his eyes. Then walks to the living room door and makes a show of peeking out of it. Peers under the tables in the living room after that.

"Well, no one here but us chickens," he says. With a co-conspirator's wink. The only corny thing from him so far. And dangles the pack again. "Help yourself. I don't see a thing."

He brandishes a silver Zippo. Which he flips open and ignites in a single, cool, one-handed gesture. We all fire up. And for twenty, singularly privileged minutes we indulge ourselves in adult vices. Staying up late. Drinking coffee. Smoking cigarettes. Watching *The Late Show* movie. And rendered all the more delicious when done with the sanction of the night watchman. Like getting permission from God to commit your favorite sins.

The next night nothing less than anarchy will do. Sweet and vertiginous. Arty gets it into his head that we will sneak out of the house. We creep out the back basement door. Steal down campus along the fields in back of the cottages. We hit the AB building. For dinchers. There are two large, canister type ashtrays just inside the door. We fish a half-dozen good-sized clips out of there.

We have no matches though. So the dining hall is next. We find an unlocked window and climb inside. Raid the pantry. For instant coffee and sugar. Then find a little locker room/office affair. We rifle through the desk drawers. Come up with a half-pack of Marlboros. A box of strike-anywhere matches. A half-dozen Styrofoam cups. And one of the curly-cue things you plug in the wall and stick into a cup of water to heat it up. My pulse is pounding when we get back outside. Every nerve in my body tingles. Every sense is at full alert. If I were familiar with the word, I would say it's like being high. When Luke comes after midnight for his break, we surprise him with coffee and cigarettes of our own.

"I'm not going to ask you where you got this stuff," he says.

A strange kind of night watchman if you ask me. I wonder aloud if he is new at this.

"About half a year or so," he tells us. "Got bored working in an office. So here I am. Least till I get bored doing this."

"Y'ever carry a gun?" Arty suddenly asks. Eyes lit up.

"God no. Nothing like that," Luke says. With wholesale distaste for the very idea. And Arty's face goes dim. "Tell ya' the truth," Luke goes on, "I'm a writer, really. Or trying to be one. Which is what I like about doing this. I get a lot of free time to myself."

I get a picture of him. Bent over a beat-up table. In the basement of some murky warehouse. Sailing into the depths of yet another silent night. At the back end of a number two pencil. A picture so familiar to me, the lonesomeness of it anyway, that it makes me ache inside.

When we get back upstairs I reach for my notebook instead of a comic. Tell Arty, when he asks, I'm writing a letter home. I sit there with a pencil. My mind wandering. The blank sheet of paper suddenly a threat and a dare. My eyes go out the window. To the spare, wintry night. Our earlier clandestine caper out there comes vividly to mind. I write:

The moon was extremely dim that night.
It was dark as I had feared.
But what have I to worry,
for I am not ascared.

I read this back a couple of times. Pleased with myself. After a minute or two I add:

I was to sleep on Willow Street.
Where there were no lights.
You couldn't see your fingers
on even the brightest nights.

The rest of it just sort of flows out. As if I am inhabiting the fiction I am concocting. About spending a night in a haunted house. No more than half an hour and I have a whole story in rhyme. When I look up from the thing I see Arty is dead to the world. I wake him up anyway. Shake him until he starts. He comes to swinging. Just misses bashing me in the eye.

"Shit!" he says when he discovers I want to read him my poem. "Fuck," he says. But he listens. Interrupting me only once. To poke his head out the locker alcove window. Share a few hawks of his mucus with the rest of the world. I follow behind him as he does this. Still reading. Not wanting to lose the flow. And finish with a flourish.

. . . I jumped out of bed so quickly
the blankets blew on the floor.
I looked around the room
then I headed for the door.
I ran and ran and ran
with nothing on my feet.
And made up my mind to never return
to frightening Willow Street.

"You just wrote that?" he says, when I'm through.

"Yup," I tell him.

Unable to keep from beaming when I say it.

He walks back to his bed and plops down. Indian style. With his legs crossed. And doesn't say anything for a minute. Just looks at me. I gape back. Wonder why I've never noticed, besides his eyelashes, how he has a scattering of freckles. So faint you can barely make them out. On either cheek.

"Read it again," he says.

And closes his eyes.

I read the thing over.

His eyes light up when I'm done.

"Cool," he says. Not a word that's traveled him-to-me before.

There's no sleep to be had after that. Edgy excitement pulses through me, in wave after wave. There is only this moment, and everything else—an entirely open book of possibilities—beyond. One of which the two of us find our way to. Just sort of wander into it. Halfway through smoking and comics and waiting for the cool night watchman to show. Both of us sprawled shoulder to shoulder on the bed. And suddenly being there that close to each other means something it hasn't before. And, one thing after another, there it is. Awkward. Curious. Everything at stake. It happens. We carry the big secret of it between us when the night watchman comes and we go downstairs. Just sit there gaping at the cowboys and Indians flickering across the TV screen.

I have a cowboy dream that night when I finally sleep. I see . . . a horse. A huge and fiery-looking beast. With steaming nostrils wide as my fists. He's tied to a tree.

"C'mon," Arty says over his shoulder. He's sitting on the horse. Giving me the funniest, drowsy-eyed look. The horse takes a few lazy steps forward. Until its backside is to me.

"Get on," Arty says. As if it is the most natural thing in the world. I have no idea how to do this. I've never ridden a horse before. But I don't want him to know I don't know how.

"C'mon," Arty says again. In a softer, moist voice. And he leans forward. To give me room in the saddle.

Somehow I get up there. Go right up the back of the horse. I have a little trouble clearing the hump of the saddle. But then slide right on. The two of us now jammed together. Like a pair of spoons. We set off. A steady trot at first. But before you know it, we are flying flat out. In giddy, breathless abandon. Pulsating with quivery, spasmodic, electric sensation. I don't know exactly what it means. Or where it will take us. But I'm definitely along for the ride.

The next day. A Saturday. Wants for words. For a change, I get Arty to follow me. Into the pines. To the spot where I come to be alone. I tell him my secret. About the listener I sometimes imagine there. The listener in the pines. He doesn't make fun of it when I tell him. Doesn't tell me I'm nuts or anything like that.

"I gotta secret, too," he tells me. "You know the thing I told ya? About my old man?" he says. Kicking in the dirt with the toe of his boot. "I guess I got kinda carried away about him owning a candy store and all. What he does is he works there. Cleans up and stuff."

I look at him. See how flushed his face is. So that I can't even see his freckles. I tell him that it's no big deal. "At least you have a father," I tell him. "At least your father's around." After that we just sit there on the pine needles for awhile. Both of us not talking out loud. Just kind of thinking our own thoughts. In a loud way. As if it might be true. That there might really be a listener there somewhere. A half hour sitting there like that. And he doesn't spit at all.

Two days later the PA speakers crackle just before the end of classes. The principal. Telling us he has good news. *Grownup good,* for my money. The strike has been settled. Tomorrow everyone will be back.

32

A Friday, a gray miserable Friday. At the end of what has seemed like a too-long week. In that stretch of miserable winter weeks following Christmas. Which have no holidays to brighten them. I wake up already drained, from not sleeping like I was supposed to the night before. I have to drag myself out of bed and down to the showers. And sloughing through the slush to breakfast is such a chore I can't even seem to drum up any wisecracks about the food when we get there. I eat breakfast daydreaming about going back to bed when I'm done.

By afternoon I feel a little better. The pace always seems to pick up after lunch. But when the bell rings and we file back upstairs to the classroom, Mr. Friedman isn't there. And the door to the classroom is locked. I put my spine against the wall and let myself slide down until I'm sitting on the floor. Friday afternoons we have history. I hate history. I've hated it since the third grade. And I'm half hoping that somehow, by some miracle or emergency, Mr. Friedman might not show. And we'll maybe get the afternoon off.

But then there he is. I see him down the corridor. He's wheeling a tall metal cart in front of him. On it is some kind of machine. A sleek, curvy, almost egg-shaped thing. Cream-colored on top and brushed silver on the bottom. Everyone crowds around the cart when he stops at the door. All I can see is the back of the thing from my spot on the floor. But I make out a word stamped on the back. A strange word. I have to struggle to pronounce it. Woll-en-sak. And struggle even more to guess what on earth a Woll-en-sak machine might do.

Mr. Friedman doesn't say anything. He just lets our curiosity burn. Digs through all manner of tinkly stuff in his trousers pocket. Comes out with his keys. Unlocks the door and wheels the cart into the classroom. He parks it next to his desk.

"Okay. Everyone in your seats," he says. "And clear your desks. Put your textbooks away."

A fair rumble ensues. Everyone gleefully yanking their desks open. Tossing in their books. Slamming the desks closed again. A minor thunderstorm.

"Okay, settle down," Mr. Friedman says and still he doesn't tell us anything about the machine. Or what it's doing here. He rests a hand on top of the thing, though. And starts telling us about a famous guy named Orson Welles. An actor. Who had a radio program in the late thirties. *The Mercury Theater* it was called. And how this guy had scared thousands of people into believing Martians were invading the earth one Halloween night. By broadcasting a live performance of a play called *The War of the Worlds* that was so realistic, a lot of people listening thought it was really happening.

"It caused mass hysteria," Mr. Friedman says.

At first I think it's a put-on. He's like that. He's not above putting one over on us sometimes. He did it to me the first day of school, as a matter of fact. He wrote his name out on the board, Herbert J. Friedman, and when I asked him what the *J* stood for he said "Otto." It cracked me up. Especially coming from him. I like when a teacher isn't serious all the time.

He's new this year, Mr. Friedman. And one by one he's had each of his students to his home for dinner. I couldn't stop acting up. The day it was my turn to go. Everything he told me don't do I did. When he told me to do something I refused. Wouldn't get in my seat when he asked me. Instead, I climbed up on one of the counters and stood there. I had no idea why. But Mr. Friedman seemed to know.

"Act up all you want," he told me. "You're not going to get out of going to my house that easy."

I calmed down after that. When we got to his house, he pulled out a deck of cards and told me to pick one. I drew the ace of clubs. Then he picked up the telephone. "Yes," I heard him say, "I'd like to speak to the swami." A few seconds went by. Then he said, "Is this the swami?" And handed me the phone. A deep and mysterious voice came through the earpiece. "One of clubs," it droned. Whatever it was I had been afraid of about going to Mr. Friedman's house, that set the tone for the evening. It was all magic after that.

For the next week I didn't give him a moment's peace. Until he showed me how he had pulled the trick off. It was simple really. All prearranged. It was his brother on the other end. And the minute he had picked up the phone he started calling off suits. Diamonds. Hearts. Spades. Etc. When he got to clubs, Mr. Friedman asked for the swami. Whereupon his brother started counting up. My card being an ace, Mr. Friedman asked if it was the swami as soon as he hit the number one. You can't imagine how privileged I felt to gain this bit of insider information. The first time I remember ever begging a teacher to teach me something.

He's been teaching me ever since.

Like right now. As he tells us about another famous guy. Who was around the same time as Orson Welles. And who also used the radio. To stir up a little mass hysteria of his own. Only this guy was in Germany. And his name was Adolph Hitler. I don't get the connection at first. Between Martians and Germans and this Hitler guy. Until Mr. Friedman tells us about the huge army Hitler had built up. Bent on taking over the world. And how they had just overrun Austria. So that when Welles made his infamous broadcast, the idea of being suddenly invaded—by the Germans at least—wasn't far from people's minds.

"So, what I thought we'd do this afternoon," Mr. Friedman says, pressing a little silver button on the side of the Woll-en-sak machine and removing the lid, "is create our own reenactment of that infamous broadcast."

Now that the lid is off, I can see that this Wollensak thing is just a tape recorder. A strange one, though. With spacey-looking, see-through dials. Which are lit by some unseen inner glow. And it has a flat, wedge-shaped microphone. *If Martians have tape recorders . . .* I think to myself, as Mr. Friedman threads a reel of tape through a series of little wheels, *they look just like that.* He pinches a curved aluminum trigger on the side. Punching a rectangular button in front at the same time. The thing springs to life.

"Testing. Testing. One, two, three," he says, holding the funny microphone close to his face. Then shuts the thing off. We are on the edge of our seats as he rewinds the tape. You could hear a pin drop, it's so quiet. A few seconds later, we hear his voice again. "Testing. Testing. One, two, three." Only deeper and more rich, now. Every click of his tongue so clear and distinct. You'd think it was God himself talking. And I think, *Wow! A machine that blows you up bigger than life.*

For the next twenty minutes or so none of us are sure of the whys and wherefores of what Mr. Friedman has us do. We play an old dance record into the microphone for a few seconds then turn it down. He starts talking into the microphone. Kind of purring into it. Like a radio announcer. "We bring you live ballroom music from the Meridian Room of the Park Plaza in New York City," he says. Then the music goes back up. After a few seconds we kill the music altogether. And he cuts back in. Only this time he's a newscaster. Interrupting the program for a special report. About three big explosions "observed" on Mars. And a mysterious flaming object that was "sighted" falling on a farm in Grover's Mill, New Jersey. "Our special commentator, Carl Phillips, has been dispatched to the scene," he says. Meanwhile, we take you back to the Meridian Room."

We go back and forth like this for a while, from music to special report to music again. Each time we cut away we get another piece of the story. Before you know it, the police and army have surrounded a huge cylinder-shaped object that has landed behind a farm in Grover's

Mill. Up until this point it's been all Mr. Friedman and the record player. But then the cylinder opens up. And once that happens we all get into the act.

Mr. Friedman speeds up the recorder. And has one of us unscrew the lid of a mason jar in front of the mike. Then, when the Martian comes out, he hauls out a huge saw. And has another kid wobble it in front of the mike. He looks kind of dumb doing this. The thing doesn't make any sound. I get the job of being one of the machine gunners. Rat-tat-tatting a pair of rulers against the edge of the desk when the army attacks the ship. It's a lot of fun. But doesn't sound much like gunfire to me. The air force comes in after this. With aerial bombs. Another kid. Standing on a chair. And dropping the big, thick Webster's dictionary on the floor. It lands with a stupid thunk! Five, ten minutes of this. Banging and thunking and so forth. And it all begins to seem kind of lame to me.

But then we play the tape back. And it's pure magic! Slowed down now, the mason jar lid sounds like an awesome slab of metal being arduously dragged back. And even though we couldn't hear the sound of the wiggling saw with our naked ears the machine picked it up. An eerie, high-pitched quiver. Which does not sound like anything of this earth. The rulers against the desk. The dictionary hitting the floor. All of it comes out sounding realer than real. The coolest thing I've ever seen in a classroom. What a machine, this Wollensak!

All weekend I can't get it off my mind. So there I am. Starting Monday morning. Begging Mr. Friedman to teach me. To show me how to use the machine. Then I can't wait to try it out. And one afternoon, I wheel it into the synagogue. Which serves as an all-purpose room when they're not synagoguing in it. Once I get there, though, and hook it up, I can't think of anything interesting to do with the thing. I put it into the *record* mode. Pick up the microphone and do the *testing, one, two, three* thing. I'm embarrassed by my voice when I play it back. Instead of emerging stern and assured. Like a person of consequence. I sound small and insignificant. I can't stand to listen. Just as I reach to stop the machine, Mr. Friedman's voice comes on. Right in the middle of a sentence. I hear ". . . the bread. And Richard Corey, one calm summer night, went home and put a bullet through his head." Then the tape goes dead.

A creepy feeling crawls up my spine. Sitting there. In the gloom of the dim room. The tape still unwinding. But silently now. Not offering any further explanation. The unholy picture of a man putting a bullet through his brain still reverberating in my head. That and the thought that the dark and grizzly words, which I don't know are part of a poem, were, in some mysterious way, somehow meant for me. Because I'm in a church for one thing. And because, even though I have no idea who this Richard Corey fellow might be, his despair is entirely tangible to me. I don't know why. But I can feel it. Sinking right down through me. Despair. Because God is watching.

I hear something behind me. A soft, shuffling noise. Then a light jingling sound. I spin around. And see Carl. The janitor. In the doorway. Leaning on his push broom. It's one of those big ones. The kind with a head almost as wide as the stick is long. He has his hand in one pocket of his faded green khakis. Ten thousand keys dangle from the other.

"'Tar you d'wen dare?" he says. His West Indian accent so thick I can hardly make out what he's saying. "'Tis dat ting you got dare, boy?"

"A Wollensak," I tell him. "A tape machine."

He just stands there for a second. Looking at me. Like Nathan the cook, Carl is part of the staff that works at the bottom of the pile. And like Nathan I can't meet his eyes for too long whenever I see him. The two of them remind me of Eddie and Hubert back home. Cookie's father and his brother. They both work at the Happiness Laundry in the flats. I'm not sure what they do there. But I can tell from the bulging muscles of their arms and chests that they must surely toil. I like them both, these two men of the house. Yet have always shuddered that I might catch the curse of their hard and threadbare existence. Carl. Nathan. Eddie. And Hubert. I can't keep my eyes on any of them for too long. Not without facing down a tidal wave of fear.

"Here," I tell Carl. Looking away. I set the machine on *record* and hold the microphone out to him. "Say something."

He hesitates for a minute. Then puts down the broom.

"Give it cheer," he tells me. Making come-hither motions with his hand.

I pass him the mike. He holds the thing in front of him and clears his throat. The next thing I know, he's singing.

Up in de mor-nin' . . .

Out on de job . . .

Work like de de-vil for me pay . . .

But dat lucky ol' sun ain't got nut-tin' to do . . .

But roll aroun' hea-ven all day.

His voice cracks on the Os at first. But by the second verse it starts coming from a deeper place. Starts to tremble with things I recognize. Pain and longing and heartbreak. Right down to the hollows of my soul.

I fuss wid my woo-man, tall wid my kids . . .

Sweat 'til I'm wrin-kled and gray.

But dat lucky ol' sun ain't got nut-tin' to do . . .

But roll aroun' hea-ven all day.

I recognize what kind of song it is, too. Even though I've never heard it before. An old slave song. I think of the pageant. The one that marked my last day at Central School. I think of old darkies pining away.

Good Lord up a-bove, can't you see I'm pi-nin'?

I got tears all in my eyes.

Send down dat cloud wid da sil-ver li-nin'.

Lift me to pa-ra-dise . . .

I think of my mother's music. Of the gospel tunes Wayne and she spend hours picking out on the old secondhand upright in the living room. Think of how the house always seemed too small when they did. How it always seemed to corner me.

Show me dat ri-va.

Take me a-cross.

Wash all me troubles a-waaay . . .

I think of weariness. Of times when you just can't drum up the strength and spirit to face it all.

But dat lucky ol' sun

ain't got nut-tin' to do

But roll aroun' hea-ven all day . . .

I think of lucky ol' sons. Of the easy glide through life they seem to own as a given. I think of Hubert. Whose room was right above where Wayne and I slept. Think of lying in my bed at night. The sound of his record player bleeding down through the ceiling. He has a big stack of Motown forty-fives. And he plays them all the time. James Brown crooning *Please Please Me.* Little Anthony telling the world how it *Hurts So Bad*. Brook Benton pining for that lonely, *Rainy Night in Georgia*. Songs of longing and heartbreak. Crowding into my room. Turning the midnight dark an inky blue. Bathing me in the brilliance of pain.

One hot, muggy, summer night I went upstairs to pee. And saw that Hubert had his door open. To beat the swelter, I suppose. And ventured quietly down the hall, when I came out of the bathroom, to sneak a peek inside. The room was dim. The only illumination coming from a red bulb. Screwed into the fixture in the center of the ceiling. It cast a benign crimson glow upon the dinginess. Imposing rough harmony upon the mismatched, secondhand odds and ends appointing the little room. Most of it draped with pieces of cloth. To conceal the erosion of hard wear.

Hubert was slumped across the bed. His shirt off. A do-rag wrapped around his head. A wisp of smoke curled from the stub of a Kool screwed into the corner of his mouth and made for the ceiling. It struck me how much he looked like a man doing time. How much his room resembled a prison cell. A place from which he would do well to make his escape. A tan and brown record player scratched and crooned in the center of the room.

When you're all alone in your lone-ly room
And there is nothing, but the smell of her per-fume
Don't you feel like cryin'?
Don't you feel like cryin'? . . .

The answer was yes. Seeing Hubert lying there. In his red-soaked one-man cell. Ticking off the moments of his life. I did feel like crying. Just as the song said. For the meager heritage reserved for chocolates like me.

I think of all of this. Not wanting to think of any of it. As Carl's voice suffers away. And when he's finished. And hands me back the microphone. When in the sudden quiet that surrounds us I look at him. At those knobby, calloused fingers. Wrapped around the stick of a broom that is newer, fresher and better cared for than he is. I think about every Lucky Richard. Every Lucky Steve. And pretty-boy Mike. Every casual, shiny-haired, lucky ol' son whose life I have ever gazed upon in envy. And it's as if I have been tracked down and caught dead to rights. There is no way, in that moment, I can at all deny the thing that has always chased me. Despite how far and how fast I have been determined to run. From any and every odd tic of defeat that lies in the heart of grown black men.

Carl gets a big, wide smile when we play the tape back. Then half-embarrassed he comes back around. Wants to know if I have permission to be here. Fooling around with school equipment in the synagogue. His eyes narrow in when I tell him I do. He asks me if I'm sure. I tell him "Yeah, I'm sure. Mr. Friedman gave me permission."

"You don' be lyin' to me now, boy," he says. With a look that goes through me like an X-ray machine. "Cause da' true have a way of finding you out."

33

Princess is long and black and sleek. And with a personality all her own. That meets the things we do with profound befuddlement. I have no idea what short-haired breed she is. A dog is a dog is a dog to me. Nor does she particularly figure directly in events here. Just that she is the house dog. Whose larder, always at least a case of Alpo, we keep stacked against the wall in the basement. Sixteen cans of which I have borrowed. And erected a kind of pyramid out of them. Five cans across at the bottom. Each spaced a couple of inches apart. Four atop of that. Then three. And so forth.

Behind this construction, which sits on the tabletop, is a large aluminum bowl. Half filled with water. And in the water is a goodly chunk of dry ice. We had ice cream for dessert at dinner tonight. And they pack it in the stuff to keep it cold. I was able to get my hands on a piece and smuggle it back to the house wrapped in a wad of napkins. As it cold boils in the bowl of water, the steam billows out. Between the spaces in my pyramid. It looks neat to me. Mysterious and mystical. Pharaoh's Tomb comes to my mind. It's Christmas Day. And there are six of us who, for one reason or another, didn't get to go home. In my case the reason was Emmett. The counselor who lives upstairs. I was coming out of the dining hall and spotted a fresh dincher. Someone had lit the thing and dropped it after a drag or two. It was still smoldering. I thought I had been cool enough about clipping it and stowing it in the pocket of my jacket. I knelt down and pretended to be tying my shoelaces. When I stood up again I heard Emmett's voice over my shoulder.

"Okay, give it here," he said.

I played dumb. But he'd seen the whole thing.

“That cigarette butt you just put in your pocket,” he said.

Emmett came to work here fresh out of the Army. A thing he’s very proud of. He keeps his hair trimmed military style. Close at the sides. And he’s forever going around in green khakis. Two days after the strike he called me aside and asked me if I knew why it was forbidden for combat soldiers to smoke in a foxhole. Which of course I didn’t know. Because you can see the glow of a cigarette two miles away, he declared. Then told me he knew me and my buddy, meaning Arty, had been sneaking cigarettes in the locker alcove at night. He’d seen the flame. Lucky thing for me that he was out on strike, he said. Adding that he’d be keeping an eye on me.

He doesn’t work at our cottage. He works the junior unit. But every now and then he’ll come back to the house a little tipsy. Weekends mostly. On his day off. And call us all down to the rec room for a “house meeting.” A rambling monologue from him, really. Part army talk. Part bromide. Part cautionary tale. But always the same stuff. “I’m not here for a popularity contest,” he must have said a dozen times. “I can be as nice as you let me be. Or as mean as you make me be.”

Catching me in the act of swiping a butt off the sidewalk was an *as-mean-as-you-can-make-me-be* kind of thing, as it turned out. He reported it to Pop Gruzman. Who reported it to who knows who in the weekly meetings that they have. Where everyone who deals with us sits down and talks about every kid. The penalty for smoking is that you lose your home visit. So here I am.

They had me call home. Dialed the number and left me alone. To give my mother the bad news. I didn’t own up to the smoking thing. Smoking is a “worldly” vice she has always told me. Which I took to mean that it was a habit indulged in by mean and evil men. “I had picked up the butt,” I told her. But as a piece of litter. With the intent of throwing it in the trash. A much less gut-grinding offense. Lying to her over the phone. She said she was sorry. That she would miss me being there. That she would bring my gifts up when she came to visit.

Her voice sounded weary when she said it. "I'll pray for you," was the last thing she said. It hit me like a slap in the face.

Now I've got the checker set. And I'm tossing them at the pyramid. Trying to see if I can get one to go between the cans. And into the bowl. It's trickier than it looks. Takes me half a dozen tries before I land one in and let off a satisfied chuckle. I notice Sudak watching me. Wonder why he hasn't gone home. He's never caused any trouble here that I know of. Certainly nothing that would cause him to lose his home visit.

I asked Mrs. Mendelsohn about this at one of our sessions. Asked what most of the kids were doing here. When they all seem so normal. She told me of course they do. That we were all normal kids. That they take in kids who are at risk. I thought, *at risk of what?* But didn't ask. And staring right at Sudak now, I still can't see it. He drops his eyes the minute I look over. And sits there contemplating the floor. His dark brown bangs hanging down his brow. His face pale and bloodless. Eyes forlorn and wistful. Waiting, it seems, for someone or something to dictate what he is to do next. I still don't get it. Even as I take in his pulpy, battered-in nose. And the pencil line of healed-over scar tissue descending his once-split upper lip. I still can't figure out at what risk this quiet, mousy kid could possibly be. And why on earth they won't let him go home.

I chuck another checker. It rattles between the cans. Lands in the bowl with a *doink*. A brassy laugh gallops out of me. And this brings up Sudak's eyes. They look wounded and solicitous at the same time. They travel the bygone trajectory of the checker I just threw. Settle on my mist-enshrouded dog-food pyramid. And putting two and two together, he meets my grin. With a tiny, nervous smile.

I scoop up a palmful of checkers. Point them his way.

"Wanna give it a try? See if you can get one between the cans?"

He doesn't. Not really. But he's not one with the stuff to tell you no. Especially if you are bigger than him. I watch him make a few half-hearted tosses. The checkers *clink* and *ding* off the sides of the cans.

He gives me a shrug when they are all gone. And tries to retreat back across the room. But I refuse to let him go.

"Try again," I tell him. "The trick is to throw them edgewise."

He sighs before going at it again. A sigh that wants to know why I am putting him through this. But gives the second try a better effort. As he does, Mike Siegel comes clattering down the stairs. His parents are away. In Washington, I think. Spying the Alpo rig. And Sudak chucking checkers at it. He makes a point of addressing Sudak, not me. Wants to know what we are up to. Next thing you know, Siegel's going at it. He gets two out of ten.

"Let's see ya' beat that," he tells Sudak.

"I'll bet you I can," I tell him.

"Shit, Stringer," he says. The first words he's condescended to say to me in the longest. "Three out of ten, you're saying."

"Yeah," I say. Then add, "For snacks. Winner take all." A thing I regret minutes later. When I fail to land even one. It goes to double or nothing. Both of us pitching now. Then spill over to an indoor ring-toss set we have hauled from the supply chest. A colorful affair. With a bright green disk, into which a short, fire-engine red upright post is inserted. And three yellow rings. The kind of cartoon hues that illuminate amusement parks. This, coupled with the fact that the three of us are within minutes completely immersed in the games we're playing, gives me an idea.

"A little like the Midway, huh?" I try. "The one at Coney Island."

Sudak nods his head. Encouragement enough for me.

"I'll bet we could put one together just like it. Just from the stuff we got down here. Look." I find a little plastic pail among the house recreation supplies. The kind you take with you to the beach. It's the color that catches my eye. A vivid orange. I put it across the room. Grab a few ping-pong balls.

"Three tries to get one in on a bounce."

No one falls at my feet over this bright idea.

But no one calls it lame either.

"What about these," Siegel says. And pulls out the archery set. A plastic bow. Three wooden arrows. With suction cup tips. And a big, bull's-eye target. Four games already. And plenty of other stuff still in the rec cabinet. There's no telling how big a thing this idea could turn into. And then I think, why just us? With a little effort. And everyone pitching in. We could transform the rec room into our own boardwalk. Just like at Coney Island. And invite the guys from the other cottages over. Everyone who's stuck here for the holidays.

Sudak lights up to this right away.

Siegel's a little more reserved.

"How would we do that, exactly?" he wants to know.

I don't have an answer. But make it up as I go along. Take the idea upstairs. Where the other three of us stuck here are yawning through Christmas Day TV programming. It doesn't take much convincing. They're up for anything. I go to Pop Gruzman next. He frowns at first. In the face of my breathless gush. But it's a thing right up his alley, after all. Making something out of nothing.

"You can do zis?" he says.

I shake my head. Not at all sure that I can.

"Okay. Go," he says. "When is ready I will call to bring za other kids."

I bellow the news as I barrel back downstairs.

"Pop says it's okay!"

A dizzying rush of activity follows. People racing up the stairs. Then thundering down them again. Clutching one unlikely object after another. Most of which, when basted in the heat of the rising creative fever, turn out to fit, one way or another, perfectly into our scheme.

A set of drinking glasses. Fill them halfway. With Kool-Aid for color. Throw in a chip of dry ice for bubbly effect. And, bingo! Our own version of Coney Island's ping-pong ball toss. A wide-mouthed trash basket. Anchor the thing with weights from the house barbell set. And the ball from the pint-sized NBA set and it becomes the basketball bounce. Get one in and win a prize! Even a stupid, plastic Playskool wind-up clock. Which someone obviously never outgrew. With its cartoon colors, a perfect timer for a brainteaser we concoct out of math flash cards from school. It's an entirely electric and contagious thing. Everyone suddenly burning with genius.

We cadge makeshift booths together, too. They rise out of thin air. All of us working flat-out. Using anything at hand. Tables. Chairs. Benches. Sawhorses and planks from the tool shed. Covering them with sheets, blankets and tablecloths. Trimming them with crepe paper, streamers and handmade signs. Then Siegel. Lugging down his most prized possessions. His hi-fi and stack of forty-fives. Asking me where I want him to put the thing. Everyone asking me. Looking for my approval! Even Zunya gets into the spirit of things. Kicks in a couple of weeks' worth of goodies and sodas from his snacks stash.

Then Emmett wanders in. With half a head on. Takes in the riotous disarray the rec room is in. Sees us all dashing about.

"Anyone want to tell me what's going on here?" he says.

"A carnival," someone says. "Pop says it's okay."

He lets this sink in. Eyes wandering the room. Draws a bead on the blanket we have suspended from the ceiling. With a gaping hole cut in the middle of it.

"I know Pop didn't give you permission to destroy school property," he says.

But it's not school property. It belongs to Siegel. It was his idea, too. Using it for a sponge toss game. The idea being for one of us to put his head through the hole. To be pelted with damp sponges. Siegal explains all this to Emmett. Who teeters slightly as he listens.

"Uh-uh," he says. "I can't let any of you kids put your head through there. Too dangerous. What if someone gets hurt?"

I hadn't thought of that.

“What about goggles?” I suggest. “Anyone got goggles?”

“I have a better idea,” Emmett says. And goes up to his room. He comes down about ten minutes later in an old t-shirt. And wearing a bathing cap.

“You're going to need to make a bigger hole,” he says. “If I'm going to get my big head through there.”

There isn't anything said. As we hustle to make the adjustment. No one wants to spook the moment. Crusty ol' Emmett offering himself up as a sacrificial lamb like this. A thing we would never even imagine imagining. It proves to be a transcendent moment. From there on everything takes on a breathless, boundless spirit of its own. That takes us into one of those rare times and places when you know that anything and everything is entirely possible. When we are done and everything stands ready, it's an almost reverent moment.

“Yeah, but what about prizes,” someone says. Mark. A curly haired kid with a raspy kind of voice. A relentlessly practical imp to boot.

“Who said anything about prizes?” Sudak says.

“Ya gotta have prizes,” Mark says back.

“Yeah,” Siegel echoes. “What's the point if you don't have no prizes.”

I hadn't thought of that either.

When the kids from the other cottages show up it's the look on their faces. The *what's-all-this-about?* frowns at the basement door. Exploding in genuine, golly-gee wonder as they mill into the room. Then flushed and pop-eyed with excitement. Then it's the voices. Shouting, laughing, screaming. Swelling and submerging on the winds of fortune. As they try their luck at this and then that. The sound of kids having fun. Thirty, forty of them. Squeezed into a room designed for less than half as many. But also the sound of kids who have made their own fun. And the biggest attraction of it all is just as Emmett had predicted. The line to whack his puss with a damp sponge arcs halfway around the room.

A manic melee. And a miracle, too. A few months ago you could hardly coax a spare Frito from the next guy down here. Now each little booth is littered with prizes. And not the usual trinkets up for grabs at your average amusement park, either. This is the kind of loot to make a kid tug at his mother's coat sleeve and try to hustle her into opening her purse. A virgin Spalding ball. A water pistol. A Parcheesi set. A Bolo Bouncer. One of those little plastic hand games where you have to get the BB inside through a maze. Comics. Posters. Records. Even a couple of Aurora car model kits. About thirty prizes in all. Every one of them donated. All six of us pitched in. Even the stingiest of the lot. No one even had to be asked.

34

There's a big buzz the next day. Everyone talking about what we pulled off. There's Sudak. Out of his shell. For now at least. Basking in the high signs he gets from some of the kids who came last night. A familiarity he doesn't often see. There's Mike Siegel. Not transformed into a bosom buddy exactly. But the scowl he usually holds for me is no longer there. There's the other guys in the house. Getting back from home. Half of them feeling cheated when they hear what went on. For having missed out on the whole thing. Even Arty. Who isn't exactly the *"me-too"* type. Managing to betray a hint of envy as he complains. "Great. You wait until 'm not here to have a big brainstorm."

There's Mrs. Mendelsohn. Seeing "leadership potential." She always has the neatest words. One for every high and low beam of behavior. There are my teachers. Going on about the knack they assume I have. For "creating something out of nothing," as they put it. There's Pop Gruzman. Whose trick with the newspaper and water has more to do with this supposed knack than anything else. And there's me. Quite beside my own self. At how well it all turned out.

There's everything that follows. Like the radio I build. Talk about making something out of nothing. A razor blade. A point from a pencil. A little wire. And an empty toilet paper roll. Is about all it takes. You don't even need even batteries. You just "ground" the thing by hooking it to a radiator pipe. Or anything else that's sunk in the ground. I read about it in a book. Have to do it myself before I'm ready to believe it can work. A foxhole radio, they call it. Because that's where they were first created. During the war.

Most of the kids here have transistor radios. Arty has a tiny one. Small enough to fit in a shirt pocket. Which he listens to by earphone at night. Once in a great blue moon I can get him to lend it to me for a short while. For the illicit pleasure of rock and roll after lights out. And Cousin Brucie chattering into my ear. But that doesn't even begin to come close to the thrill I get when that first scratch of static comes in on my homemade rig. Followed by the Drifters. Singing *Save the Last Dance for Me.* A feeling of near cosmic potency. That anything and everything is entirely possible. All that's needed is to go all out for it. Like scratching out a double on an infield blooper that time.

. . . Then there's the rest of the school year. During which everything seems to confirm this notion. I submit my foxhole radio as a science project and get an A. It's a big hit when we have our science fair, too. I show my rhymes to my English teacher. Eight of them in all by the time I work up the courage. She likes them so much she has them published. A neat-looking little book. Done by the print shop on campus. One rhyme to a page inside. An inkbottle, a quill and a scroll of parchment on the cover. And my name there at the bottom. In classic Roman type. Like the name of a person of consequence.

Best of all is the bright smile it draws from my mother. When she and Wayne come to visit and I spring the book on them. "You've got a gift," she says. Beaming so wide her nose expands and her glasses ride up on her face. My eyes go right to Wayne when she says it. Remembering how Mama had cried the same thing to him. Wayne, being Wayne, puts up a big effort of making nothing of it. Settles his glasses back on his nose with a knuckle. Nods his head and keeps eating. Funny thing is, it doesn't bother me as much as it might have. I am pretty much able to shrug the snub off. I almost chuckle, in fact.

I take up art class. Because I like the teacher. Mac Greenfield. Who never wears a tie. Is always in wrinkled clothes. And is kind of absent-minded to boot. A real artist, to my eyes. A little like visiting a favorite uncle every day, being in his class. And with him you can choose whatever kind of art you want to do. You just sort of fumble along until you hit a wall. Then you raise your hand for Mac.

With me it is drawing hands. They keep coming out looking like a loose bag of sausages. Mac doesn't teach me how to draw them, exactly. It's just something he knows. Something he can do. He takes my pencil from me. And, half a dozen strokes with the thing on a piece of scrap paper, there it is. But no word on how he did it. As if it were in the pencil all along. Just waiting for him to release its flow. The best I can do is hope to imitate some of his moves.

In English class there is a trip to see *West Side Story*. Which I'm not all that excited about at first because I'm no big fan of musicals. I can't see the sense of interrupting a story to sing a song. But none of that seems to bother me with this show. The music stays with me even more than the story. I walk around singing *Maria* for days after. Belting it out as I tool around the house. Until Mrs. Gruzman stops me one afternoon. "No, no, Cav-a-lee," she tells me. "Not so loud. Is a love song. You must sing it soft. Romantic." She swoons with her eyes when I try it again. *Sotto voce*, this time.

That next week I do my first painting. By trial and error mostly. A watercolor. Of a knife fight. In an alleyway. It's *West Side Story* all the way. Mac has to help me with the hands. It sells right away when we have a showing for the public midway through the school year. They buy three of my paintings in all. One of which gets framed and hung on the wall of the infirmary. A good case of the sniffles or whatever, and I get to visit with it.

Meanwhile the dynamic between Arty and me does a gradual flip-flop. I see an ad for a battery-operated tape recorder in the back pages of one of his comics. And harass my mother about getting me one. For weeks. Every time she comes up to visit. When she finally does, I use the thing to bring Arty's comics to life. Acting them out. Adding sound effects. And music. Just like Mr. Friedman did with the Wollensak. Next thing you know, I've got Arty hooked into doing them with me.

It becomes the thing we do when we have free time. Instead of making mischief. Or trying to kill squirrels in the pines. And, one thing after another, doing this, a different Arty starts to emerge. The big chip he always has on his shoulders begins to come down. He discovers he can laugh, too. And have fun.

Somewhere in there. All this going on. Five directions at once. I start to change. I don't notice it myself. Don't know if this happens along a gradual curve or all at once. It takes Mrs. Mendelsohn to point it out to me. Once she mentions it, though, I know it's true. I don't know how or why exactly. But I can see it. By some trick or hook it's gotten to be. That I'm just not so angry any more.

"Tell me," Mrs. Mendelsohn says. Right out of the blue one day. "How would you feel about going home for good?"

"Home?" I say. Surprised. Wondering, as I say it, exactly when it was that getting to go back home had ceased to be an ever-present ambition.

"Maybe at the end of the school year?" She says. "How would you feel about that?"

I tell her it would be just great. At the same time, I feel a tug. For camping in the woods. For trips to Coney Island. For winning ribbons in the Maccabeah. For all the fun things of the summer here. And more than anything, a tug for all the kids here to do them with.

"Well, then," Mrs. Mendelsohn says. "Just keep up as you're doing and we'll see what we can do."

That next week I make something out of nothing yet again. I get into it with one of the kids from Mr. Riccimini's class. Mr. Riccimini's a little guy. I'm half a head taller than him. And when he intervenes on the kid's behalf, that other someone or something I had thought was long gone leaps out of me. Dares to take a poke at Mr. Riccimini's belly. Only to find he's like iron down there. And no one's pushover. Two, three seconds later he has me pinned on the floor. Everyone crowded around. Scratching their heads. It's another week and a half before my disposition starts to even out again. A thing that does not escape Mrs. Mendelsohn's notice.

"So!" she chirps when I see her a week later, "excited about going home?" She's a little too bright when she says it. Her smile a little forced.

I tell her *yeah.*

"And what are your plans?" she hums.

"Plans?" I say back.

"For the summer," she says. As if it's the most obvious thing in the world.

I shrug.

Plans? What kid plans his summer?

"Well, how do you usually spend your summers?"

I tell her about the lot across the street. About Chuck and Michael and me hanging out there. About Harbor Island. The beach that lies at the foot of the town. About the fireman's carnival they have down there every year, too. About Playland Amusement Park in Rye. She frowns it all away.

"Doesn't sound very structured, I'm afraid," she says. The back end of a pencil to her lips now. "What about camp? Or summer school? Have you considered either one of those?"

"Not really," I tell her. Thinking, *why would I sign up to go to some place else after just getting out of here?* "Just summer stuff. You know. Go out and play and all that."

"I don't know," she worries. "I'm a little concerned about having you in an unstructured environment. After all the progress you've made."

I don't know what to say to this. So I just sit there.

"Tell you what," she says. And consults her watch. "Why don't we talk this through some more. When you come next week."

I can already see the writing on the wall. We'll talk about it next week. And the week after that. And the week after that. I ask her if it was the thing with Mr. Riccimini.

"I don't know how all that happened," I tell her. And she studies me very closely when I say it. Then she sighs.

"You've been here for what? About two years. Settling back into home life again can take some real adjustment. You won't have the kind of intensive support you're used to getting here. I'm worried about you wandering around all summer without anything constructive to do. It could be asking for trouble."

I want to tell her, *I won't be wandering around.* But I don't.

"I'm thinking it might be better, on second thought, to wait a couple of months. Until school starts again. You could go home then. How would you feel about that?"

I don't answer. I just sort of raise my hand halfway. Then lose the momentum. Mrs. Mendelsohn has a word for this, too.

"It's quite natural to feel a little ambivalent," she says.

I have to look it up. And find some comfort when I do. That there is an official word for feeling different than you are supposed to feel. That it's not an unheard-of thing.

We have graduation in the synagogue. All of us melting in our suits and ties. A long, drawn-out drudgery to me. With the sun outside. Calling. When they get to the esses, though, I perk up. A little thrill goes through me when they call my name. Walking up to get my diploma I hear cheers. From my friends. More of them now than ever. And then another surprise. A special "Citizenship Award." Engraved on a scroll. And signed by the director. Just for me. My fingers tremble when I reach to take it. I can barely clear the frog in my throat to say thank you.

There is a prom. Outside. In the area by the pool. A catered affair. Balloons and music and refreshments. Under the night sky. I nudge around in my dress clothes. Entirely too shy to ask any of the girls to dance. Not that I know how to in the first place. Except for maybe the twist. Halfway through the thing, though, one of the girls walks up to me. A Greek girl. Named Kris. With fiery hair. That runs black and gold and rust. "C'mon," she says. And pulls me out to the dance floor. A slow dance, too. I stomp all over her feet like a clod. Red-faced with apologies. But she doesn't seem to mind. "You'll get the hang of it," she says.

When the music stops she gives me a peck on the lips. My first real kiss from a girl. And suddenly I'm not a kid anymore. I walk over to Mr. Riccimini. Back arched. Shoulders straight. And in words that just seem to be ready and waiting to be spoken, apologize to him. Man to man.

About the Author

Lee Stringer is the author of the acclaimed *Grand Central Winter: Stories from the Street* (Seven Stories Press, 1998; Washington Square Press, 1999), which chronicled his twelve years of homelessness in New York City. *Grand Central Winter* has been translated into eighteen languages and was both a *New York Times* Notable Book and one of the Top Ten Recommended Titles of the Year in *USA Today.* He is also the author, with Kurt Vonnegut, of *Like Shaking Hands with God: A Conversation About Writing* (Seven Stories Press 1999; Washington Square Press, 2000). For three years in the mid-1990s Stringer served as a senior editor of *Street News,* eventually becoming editor-in-chief. In 1996, he sought treatment and recovery for drug addiction at Project Renewal.

His recent writing has appeared in *The Nation* and the *New York Times* among other publications, and in the collections *Empire City: New York Through the Centuries* (2002), *Unholy Ghosts: Writers on Depression* (2001), *The Time Out Book of New York Walks* (2000), *The Way Home: Ending Homelessness in America* (1999), and *The Man with the Golden Arm: Fiftieth Anniversary Critical Edition* (1999). Stringer's commentaries can be heard on NPR's *All Things Considered.* He currently serves on three nonprofit boards: Project Renewal in New York City, the Friends of the Mamaroneck Library, and the Youth Shelter Program of Westchester. He lives in Mamaroneck, New York, where he grew up.